Lotus Elise

Other Titles in the Crowood AutoClassics Series

Lotus Elise

The Complete Story

John Tipler

CROWOOD
AutoClassic

First published in 1999 by
The Crowood Press Ltd
Ramsbury, Marlborough
Wiltshire SN8 2HR
www.crowood.com

This impression 2003

British Library Cataloguing-in-Publication Data
A catalogue record for this book is available from the British Library.

ISBN 1 86126 213 2

Typeset by Textype Typesetters, Cambridge

Printed and bound in Great Britain by the Bath Press

Contents

Acknowledgements

The Elise has been a treat to write about, not merely because it is such a brilliant car, but because the people at Lotus have been friendly and courteous throughout. I should like to extend my gratitude to the Lotus public relations department for setting up the meetings that enabled me to carry out most of the research for the book. In particular, thanks to Pruneliar Stuart and Alastair Florance who co-ordinated the project within Lotus, as well as Carol Highmoor and publicity manager Karen Angus. I am delighted to have had the Foreword written by that personable double act, Julian Thomson and Richard Rackham.

On the production side, thanks indeed to Luke Bennett, manufacturing engineering manager, for the detailed guided tour of the whole factory and help with composing captions for pictures of the build process. Manufacturing manager Morris Dowton provided the longer view of Lotus production, being a veteran of the Cheshunt days – and thanks very much for the company tie, Morris!

Product engineering manager Tony Shute provided initial guidance and valuable insights into the philosophy behind the Elise and its gestation period, as did Ben Wright. Julian Thomson was head of Lotus Design, and as such was responsible for designing the car's wonderful shape, and he described the styling process and the heartaches that involved. His close friend and colleague Richard Rackham was responsible for the design of the chassis and suspension, and talked at length about engineering issues tackled and overcome during the productionizing process.

Stephen Swift, chief engineer on chassis development, and Lotus executive engineer Dave Minter spoke about the major task of honing the ride and handling, while John Miles provided full details of the damping set-up. Alastair McQueen gave an expansive demonstration of what the Elise was capable of around the Lotus test track. Neil Lloyd was chief engineer on the GT1 sports racing car project, and he and Richard Rackham reminisced about the trials and tribulations of the undertaking and its incredible sleep-depriving deadlines.

I am very grateful for the loan of the Elise press cars, and my impressions are recorded in Chapter 6. To get a different slant on the Elise's versatility, Dave Minter put the Elise Sport '190 Motorsport' car though its paces to show me what it could do on the track.

Alan Blizzard at Hydro Raufoss Automotive UK organized pictures of the extrusion manufacturing process and supplied background information on his company. Thanks also to Pete Bullivant-Clark and Bob Mustard of Hydro Raufoss. Lotus's other suppliers were equally helpful. John Gibbs at Rover supplied details and pictures of the K-series power unit and its selection for the Elise, while Arno Stapersma of Koni Shock Absorbers provided details of his products.

Tom Wood of the National Motor Museum, Beaulieu, took the Hethel production line pictures and some dramatic test track photographs. Archive shots were very kindly provided by Jon Day at Beaulieu and by **Pruneliar** Stuart at Lotus Cars Ltd. Shots of the press cars were taken by Tom Wood in the Beaulieu studio, by my wife Laura at UEA and in Norwich, by Derek Hibbert at Prescott hillclimb, and Mike Valente was good enough to furnish shots of the car's 1995 Frankfurt debut, while the Italian race series pictures are by Claudio Signori. And I took some snaps of the press and Motorsport cars.

The majority of the text for the book was written up while I was staying at the Quinta da Eira Velha, a vineyard in the dramatic port wine country of northern Portugal, for which many thanks to Peter and Richard Newman. No shortage of hairpin bends and demanding roads in the Douro. Now there's a place to drive an Elise! Finally, I want to dedicate this one to my eldest son Julius.

With heavily revamped bodywork, the Motorsport Elise was announced at the 1999 Earl's Court Show. It was the basis of a one-make race series that became part of the BTCC support package for 2000, and featured at certain international circuits such as Spa-Francorchamps. Its aerodynamic composite bodywork had a high downforce front splitter and adjustable rear wing, plus a modified engine cover and air scoop to aid cooling. It was powered by the 203bhp 1,795cc four-cylinder twin-cam unit allied to a Quaife straight-cut close-ratio five-speed gearbox with Motorsport driveshafts.

Foreword

To be asked to design a Lotus is an honour and a rare privilege, but to be given the task with a clean sheet of paper and virtually no briefing is an opportunity that happens only once in a designer's life-time.

Our personal relationship has developed over many years, through shared appreciation of the finer things in life, such as Italian motorbikes and sports cars; we've egged each other on through attempts at extreme sports and other outdoor pursuits, some successful, some not. We've even served as best man at each other's weddings. But our work disciplines of engineering and design had seldom crossed until the advent of the Elise.

Designers and engineers are normally from opposite ends of the spectrum, and uniting them can be an arduous and frustrating task. Their approach to problems often contrasts wildly, and their arrival at completely different solutions is not unheard of. Trying to get them to agree on a successful outcome can be impossible. In short, designers and engineers mix like champagne and sump oil.

However, the marriage between designers and engineers can be an extremely harmonious one: bring in strong support from development and manufacturing departments and the results can prove to be outstanding – witness the Sony Walkman, the Ducati 916, the Porsche 911 and Lotus's own original Elan. All are tributes to the magic formula, and all have become true icons of their kind. Dare Lotus assume to have produced an icon in the Elise? Only time will tell.

So for us the Elise was more than just another project – it was the opportunity to work together in a professional capacity and give our friendship the ultimate

The contours of the Elise were the inspiration of Julian Thomson, who was Lotus's head of design.

Richard Rackham was lead chassis design engineer on the Elise.

challenge. The opportunity came about through great fortune – we were being asked to design a car that we ultimately desired! Needless to say, we poured our souls into it. There was more on the line for us than our professional reputations. We were not alone in our enthusiasm, and the spirit and dedication from all involved was unequalled by any project either of us had ever worked on. It can only be expected that, with the tremendous reception of the Elise, several will be stepping forward to take credit for the concept. Perhaps the most often asked question at Lotus is: 'Whose idea was it?'

There is only one individual whose vision and philosophy are inherent within the Elise and who can truly be the man behind her and her success. The Lotus Elise is now the most successful Lotus to date, perhaps because it is the most 'Lotus' Lotus ever, and the man who should take the credit is of course our founder Colin Chapman. The Elise embodies the most purist contemporary interpretation of the Chapman philosophy of elegant engineering and innovative application. Chapman criticized the 'old school' engineers by stating that 'the trouble with experts is they know what can't be done'. The Elise team battled against the old school, just as Chapman had before them, and maintained the opinion that simplicity was the key. Complex design solutions are ironically very easy; unclouded, clean design is in fact the real challenge.

So, by returning to its core values Lotus is back on the track with the Elise blazing the trail. And as for us? Well let's say we're trailblazing our own separate career paths, but our friendship is stronger than ever. The Elise has been a success in more ways than one, and along with the rest of the team, we are honoured to have been involved in what we hope will become an important landmark in the history of Lotus.

Richard Rackham and Julian Thomson
1998

Introduction

In manufacturing terms alone, the Elise was a tremendous coup for Lotus, in that it productionized a number of revolutionary ideas in car construction. It is difficult to think of another company that could have done it, and in the same time frame too – its gestation was a matter of two years, which speaks volumes about the talent and enthusiasm of the Lotus designers and workforce.

Several fundamental new concepts were incorporated in the design, which needed to be initiated and then nurtured as the project got under way. Hindsight tells us that it was all accomplished remarkably swiftly, inside three years from conception to launch, but there were innumerable hurdles to be cleared along the way. Not least were problems of sourcing and supply of components, and the project climaxed amid acrimonious internecine boardroom battles. In fact, that Project M1-11 (it was so named because it was Lotus type number 111) happened at all is a considerable achievement.

The long-running Esprit, introduced in 1975, continues to go from strength to strength, but historically Lotus's best car was the Seven. Colin Chapman's basic concept, which offered racing car handling at production car – or kit-car – prices, endures in the Caterham and a host of imitators. Within the company, many people see the Elise as a direct reference to Chapman's first principles. The original idea for the Elise was to go back to the company's roots, where light weight and simplicity were the keys to performance rather than sheer power. Caterham and Westfield plough the same furrow, making

The Lotus Eleven's aerodynamic and curvaceous shape virtually enclosed the wheels, and like today's Elise it was typical of Colin Chapman's innovative thinking. Its career spanned the 1956 and 1957 seasons, including Le Mans and sports racing events, and it was superseded by the similarly shaped 15 and 17.

Historically, the Seven was probably Lotus's best car. This 1969 series 3 model is the rare Seven S, which had a plush interior and 120bhp 1,600cc Holbay engine. Its original log book was signed by John Miles.

subtle improvements all the while and, in Caterham's case, variations like the C21. But perhaps nowhere is performance motoring so finely tuned and so state-of-the-art as in the world of super-sports motorcycles. Rivalry between the four big Japanese producers has always been intense, and alterations, updates and innovations are more readily introduced in the smaller-scale engineering milieu of bikes. One of Chapman's most frequently repeated quips was that he visualized the Seven as 'a four-wheeled motorbike', and the metaphor holds good today, for it was from motorcycles that much of the inspiration for the Elise sprang.

When you're out on a sports motorcycle, you are acutely aware of every single nuance of road surface, the optimum line through every bend – which matters, because unlike a modern car that forgives to a major extent, to get it totally wrong on a bike guarantees high-siding into the scenery. Most other functions on a bike are closer to the surface: throttle response, the shift system, and sensations like balance, weight distribution and perception of the road, not to mention the hazards of other vehicles, are far more acute than in a car – even a Seven. It's no surprise then to discover that the (former) head of design and chassis engineer, Julian Thomson and Richard Rackham, share a passion for Italian motorcycles.

When I was concluding my book on the Seven in the mid-1990s, Caterham

Just like a super-sports motorcycle, the Elise controls are instantly accessed. Thus throttle response, gear shift, balance and perception of the road are far more acutely experienced than in almost any other road car.

The Elise's transverse-mounted mid-engine configuration defines its polar moments of inertia and its roll axis, as well as raising questions to do with distribution of mass over the rear wheels. Lotus's chassis engineering experts resolved all these issues, and the Elise showcases their talents.

announced the curvaceous 21 model, and it is tempting to see the Elise as Lotus's answer to the Caterham 21. There is no question that the Elise is a revival of the minimalist Seven philosophy, brought bang up to date with Richard Rackham's pioneering chassis. But on the other hand, there is no doubt that Thomson's styling for the Elise would pass as a sports-racing car from the late 1960s.

Those of us of a certain age will immediately recognize motifs from that halcyon decade: the Ginetta G12, the Lotus 23, Lola T70, Chevron B8; there are tiny elements of the Elise's curvaceous body which remind us of these classics. No wonder then that designer Thomson's own classic car is a Ferrari 246 Dino – it is also related stylistically to the Ferrari 250LM and the glorious Ferrari 330P4 Group 6 sports prototype, and there are a handful of similarities visible in the Elise. The proportions are rather different, but the hallmarks are there, and are brilliantly done. As a member of one of those obnoxious teenage gangs weaned in the sixties on The Who and the Stones, I used

to pile off to Brands and Snetterton most weekends to thrill to the antics of such cars in events like the BOAC 500. Today, people like me and my gang who grew up in that era are potential customers for the Elise. Therefore the Elise had to be good news for the Lotus marketing department's sales forecasts.

But if it looks like an updated version of a thirty-year old Lotus, how far has the Elise actually moved on? To give you an indication, I'll toss in a few anecdotes from those bygone days, which might help make the point. From 1972 to 1975, I co-ran the John Player Special-sponsored 'JPS' Motor Sport Press Office, alongside Grand Prix statistician Mike Doodson. Our job was to follow the fortunes of Team Lotus and the F1 circus around the Grand Prix circuits, dishing out press handouts, cigarettes and stickers to journos and race fans, and our office hack was an appropriately liveried black-and-gold Elan Plus 2. Unfortunately, 'hack' was the right description, as it was usually in all sorts of mechanical trouble. For example, I was once obliged to drive from Player's Nottingham HQ to Dover in

The mid-engined Ginetta G12 was prominent in sports GT racing at club level during the mid-1960s. There are obvious similarities of detail design with the Elise, including the headlight housings and air scoops in the rear bodywork.

pouring rain with no wipers, and another time, on the motorway at night, the lights drooped ever lower the faster I went, apparently the result of a crack in the pneumatic channels. My personal transport at the time was an Elan S4 SE, an attractive car that, while truly electrifying to drive, was only marginally more reliable than the Plus 2 model described above, and was frequently to be seen with its bonnet raised or up on a ramp somewhere.

That seems to exemplify the Lotus cars of those days, but today's innovative engineering and neat styling goes hand in

hand with improved reliability that is light years away from the Elise's stylistic ancestors. This was in no small part due to the adoption of the tried and tested 1.8-litre Rover K-series twin-cam engine, which provided enough power for sports car motoring combined with efficiency and dependability. With complete justification then, the Elise was greeted with rave reviews, and the motoring press continues to deliver unanimous plaudits. And, not surprisingly, it was selected by the Design Council to appear as one of the exhibits in the Millennium Dome as a paragon of

The power unit selected for the Elise was the transverse-mounted, all-aluminium fuel-injected 1,796cc Rover K-series twin-cam engine, which provided a reliable 118bhp.

engineering excellence. My own modest and hopefully not-too-gushing appraisal of the car can be found later on in Chapter 6.

The Elise also served to showcase the talents of Lotus Engineering, who derived considerable publicity and consultancy business from its success, but the implications of its creation went further. Elise-based technology allowed Lotus to move into other spheres, and in late 1997 Zytec Engineering had just produced the first Elise-based electric supercar. It was basically the Frankfurt show car, fitted with an electric motor sufficiently powerful to take it from 0 to 90mph in around 10 seconds. As fast as a petrol-engined model, in fact, which ought to be good enough for most people. When asked what he thought of it at the BBC *Tomorrow's World* show at the NEC, Damon Hill observed that its lack of noise might well be a plus point, although there was a long way to go in terms of electric car development. 'If you didn't have people playing around with cars like this, you wouldn't know what was possible,' he said. The same is true of the standard Elise, and it is ample testimony to the talents and ingenuity of people like Richard Rackham, Steve Swift and Dave

Minter who 'played around' with the Elise that make it such a good car.

One more thing. If it hadn't been for Romano Artioli appearing on the scene and buying the company when he did, there wouldn't have been any Lotus Cars, let alone a Lotus Elise. The way things looked, the company would have been sold to a buyer who wished only to keep the engineering side of the business. The Elise was Artioli's baby and it was he who enabled it to be built in the first place.

With the Elise, Lotus productionized several ground-breaking concepts in automotive manufacturing in a relatively short time, including the bonded aluminium chassis and metal matrix brake discs, going from renderings to production in just three years.

1 Lotus: an Overview

Few car factories are so comprehensively buried in the heart of the countryside as Lotus is. Although there are big brown signposts directing traffic from the main A11 and A140, the back roads via East Carleton and Hethel give nothing away. The surrounding countryside is, for the most part, typically flat south Norfolk arable land.

The Lotus factory consists of a conglomeration of aircraft hanger-sized buildings, some old and some new, plus a smattering of portacabins. And as I compiled the book during numerous visits in 1998, construction of the new research and development buildings was in full swing on an adjacent site. When you arrive at the factory there's the inevitable sentry box in the drive, where you pause and sign in. Because there's a high degree of secrecy

about Lotus Engineering's automotive consultancy work, nobody gains admittance without first undergoing considerable scrutiny.

Beyond the factory is the test track, a boomerang-shaped circuit that was the home of a USAF Liberator squadron in the Second World War. When Lotus moved from Cheshunt in November 1966, Colin Chapman was attracted by the possibilities of flying to and from his factory, and he even orientated the flag-bedecked single storey admin office block and its gardens to face the test track-cum-airfield. A confirmed aviator, he visualized a future where air travel would be so commonplace that most visitors to the factory would actually arrive by plane or helicopter.

It had taken me over a year to gain access to the factory, which was doubly

The Lotus reception area, staffed here by Julia Godfrey. There is usually a Lotus of some sort or cutaway engine on display here – even the fabulous bicycles are featured – and the Elise Sprint in the foreground is the concept car shown at the NEC in October 1996. Its deflection screen is based on that of the classic Lotus 23 sports racer.

Senior development engineer Tony Shute oversaw the Elise M1-11 project from start to finish; he is concerned with new product development and identifying markets, as well as solving current technical problems.

frustrating as, by coincidence, I live a mere quarter of an hour's drive from Hethel. By contrast, other companies that I've written about, such as Triumph Motorcycles, TVR, Morgan and Caterham, have provided instant access. It wasn't that the Lotus hierarchy was complacent about having a book written on the Elise, because, actually, no other manufacturer I've written about has gone to the same lengths as Lotus to ensure that everything that needed to be said about the Elise and its development was accurately recorded. In

the first place, though, I had to convince them of my credentials, and the various departments within the firm – sales and legal as well as vehicle production – had to be amenable to having the book written. Thus, on my first appointment, it was with some trepidation that I climbed up to the sentry box and gave my name. Was it on the security guard's list? Had the PR people forgotten, or changed their minds after all? No, there it was, and evidently all was well. At last my foot was in the door.

My introductory meeting was with Tony Shute, the Elise project manager, who gave me a tour of the Lotus assembly lines, and his abundant smiles enabled me to relax into the subject. He explained:

> Probably over the last eighteen months I've met many of the chief executives of the car industry throughout Europe and the rest of the world, to get them to come to Lotus to look at the Elise. That's because it's quite significant as an example of how to manufacture a low-volume niche product, and as the car industry moves forward, even the big players like Ford are producing more and more niche vehicles, albeit at a higher volume. Some of these are going into subsets, which are actually no more high volume that the Elise. There are issues in Elise production that are relevant to their type of manufacturing, and there was considerable interest on the part of the car makers in the short time frame that Lotus was able to productionize the Elise, which was just over two years.

Evidently, all aspects were scrutinized, from management structure to decision-making to development phases, and, as a result, Lotus Engineering gained new business from firms that were keen to see how it was done. Although the Lotus production strategy may not necessarily be relevant to a major manufacturer, it proves that the job can actually be done, and potential clients can see that Lotus has all the systems in place to create its own products. There are only two manufacturers that make cars and have an automotive engineering consultancy: Porsche and Lotus. No other consultancies have actually created their own vehicles – firms like Pininfarina have made prototypes and rolling bodyshells for Fiat, Peugeot, Ferrari and Alfa, but have not seen the entire vehicle from concept through to production.

One of the points Lotus are making with the Elise is that it demonstrates that the company is a trend-setter – as it always was during its formative years under Colin Chapman. The company believes that sports cars have an important role to play, and are not antisocial vehicles. For example, the Elise is fuel efficient, returning 40mpg, which is better than most cars; and although the engineers missed the target weight of 1,540lb (700kg), the performance is better than anticipated because of the car's superb traction. Production volume is potentially 5,000 a year, and in early 1998 it was running at 3,300 units.

Group Lotus is made up of two companies that operate side by side. Lotus Cars Ltd builds the Elise and the Esprit, while the far larger Lotus Engineering is the consultancy for the automotive industry. The key is that both elements can operate and survive on their own, yet have a good relationship with one another and are very profitable as well. As the Esprit evolved over the years, the two groups perhaps drifted apart, but the Elise programme was so innovative that it brought both sections together again.

Other companies that became involved with the Elise project benefited as well. The firm brought into the venture to make

Front and rear clamshells are fully assembled before they are attached to the vehicle. At this point they are one move up in the cycle, which is of 36 minutes duration.

the Elise chassis was Hydro Aluminium, whose core business is the building industry, specializing in high-rise developments. Normally, the company measures the success of its business in terms of its monthly through-put of aluminium tonnage; it therefore had to embrace a change of philosophy, as extruding a high tonnage of aluminium was at odds with the lightweight concept of the Elise structure. Hydro were driven by a desire to become involved in the motor industry, and collaboration with Lotus over the Elise was a means of showcasing their wares to the world. More significant for Hydro was that

Some people use pistons or induction trumpets as desk-tidies, but at Lotus the Elise aluminium pedal extrusion is a popular alternative. Richard Rackham wanted to make them into telephone handsets to demonstrate the versatility of extrusions.

they were obliged to meet and better certain automotive industry standards, so had to run their manufacturing business with process control. Quality control is replaced by process capability, and of necessity this includes the way the inspection department is run. This department ensures that the process is capable of doing its job, and had to be monitored by Lotus during the design phase. It ensured that Lotus Engineering quickly absorbed lessons in technologies that it was new to, such as extrusions and bonding. Tony Shute comments:

> That's not to say that we shall see Lotus Cars making its own extruded aluminium chassis, because like Caterham, its business is focused on vehicle assembly. For chassis manufacture to become part of the core business, Lotus would need to be making maybe a quarter of a million units a year. And then we'd be very good at it. But just making 2,000 chassis a year wouldn't be cost-effective.

Hydro Aluminium's Tonder plant in southern Denmark, where the Elise chassis was originally made, contained two facilities. One was a noisy place like a car plant, where they chopped up bits of aluminium and welded them together with the attendant sparkling spectacle. The other was as clinical and tranquil as a laboratory, populated by white-coated technicians involved in bonding extrusions together. The former workshop was where the chassis for the Renault Sport Spider was made, the latter was the Elise chassis manufacturing area. And to the credit of Hydro Aluminium, Lotus had no idea that the Danes also had the contract to make the Renault chassis.

A number of factors caused Lotus to alter their thinking on the Elise project quite early on. Firstly, they wouldn't have been able to meet the weight target by going for a welded chassis. By implication, the weld actually reduces the strength of the aluminium, requiring thicker material to compensate for this. Also a weld unites only a seam, whereas a chemical bond joins two sections together with a patch. In any case, the motor industry that represented many of Lotus Engineering's potential clients was far more interested in the possibilities of bonded structures. It was therefore in Lotus's interests to prove that bonding a chassis was viable. Equally, it was in Hydro Aluminium's interest to show that they could manufacture it.

The crucial point is that the two designs – Renault and Lotus – were completely different. It is not possible to take the Renault chassis and simply bond it, and vice-versa. By September 1998, however, production of the Sport Spider chassis had diminished to about three units a week, underlining the fact that it was always intended to be a limited run, and perhaps confirming that Lotus had gone the more prudent route by choosing to have the Elise chassis bonded. The bonded chassis gives it its low weight, and there are other factors too: the Elise is more practical, with full weather protection that the Renault doesn't have.

While some Lotus people were sceptical of the Renault Sport Spider, Tony Shute was decidedly upbeat:

It actually started as a racing car, and at the last minute they decided to make it as a road car. Had they been asked to make a car like the Elise, no doubt they'd have done it differently. But what Alpine did was very good, because they had different constraints, and for part of the Renault empire to produce something as radical as that was admirable really. I admire the look of it, and its got some lovely details.

CORE VALUES

Tony went on to discuss the concept of the Elise design.

The Elise goes back to the core values of

Lotus, which is achieving high performance through low mass. At the beginning of 1994 Lotus recognized the opportunity for a car that would weigh less than 700kg [1,540lb], which was beyond the scope of the mainstream manufacturers, and indeed, there was nothing on the market with a target weight of that amount. Also it was felt that the niche was wide open for a real sports car rather than an adaptation of a touring car. It needed to be uncompromised, lacking all the 'bells and whistles' of a touring car derivative. The exception was the Caterham Seven – which was originally a Lotus, of course.

The original concept of the vehicle was that it would be a replacement for the second-generation Elan, which would be redundant after the 800 spare engines were used up. A follow-on model was needed rather urgently. However, financial resources and manpower were limited, and could be expressed at the time in terms of the cost of the Daimler-Benz stand at the Frankfurt Show!

The time scale was very restricted – just two years from a clean sheet of paper to production, but although they did overrun, it wasn't by much. The key was to lift the research budget from Lotus Engineering, with the proviso that the Elise would be an engineering technology showpiece for the Engineering division that would win further consultancy business for the company. The solution was to produce a simple, lightweight car, a back-to-basics vehicle that would be quite different from cars like the MGF and Alfa Romeo Spider, nice cars though they may be. Lotus describe them as 'touring cars', not real sports cars. The thinking at this stage was about what could be left out, as Tony explained:

The aim was to achieve high performance through low mass, and in this respect the Elise design goes back to the core values of Lotus. The target was to make a car weighing less than 1,540lb (700kg), and that was far beyond the scope of major manufacturers.

If the car doesn't need it, it doesn't need designing. That helps reduce both cost and weight immediately. We then start seeing performance from low mass, not through exotic and expensive powertrains. The K-series engine is also frugal and fuel efficient.

The technology required was to demonstrate our ability in the design of aluminium structures, and to prove the success of symbiotic partnerships. Lotus recognised that many companies have expertise in new technologies, not neces-sarily allied to the automotive business, and they need a platform from which to launch their products. They perceived that the Elise might well prove to be the vehicle to provide that platform. The proviso was that the technology employed had to be scaleable, so that clients of the magnitude of General Motors or Daimler-Benz could adopt it for their own vehicles, which mass use of an exotic technology like carbon fibre would preclude. Therefore any new materials used had to be classified as relevant and saleable before they could be entertained. Equally, they had to bear in mind that the vehicle they produced would be marketable, and that they would be manufacturing 750 units a year, and a total of just 2,500 units.

The whole of the engineering costs for all the new technology had to be written off on that number of cars, as well as making a profit on a sub-£20,000 car. That was a big challenge.

To begin with there was some difficulty in defining the nature of the chassis. Was it a spaceframe? No. Was it a tub? Possibly. It was always going to be made of aluminium whatever its definition. In design, it consists of two high-sided members running down either side of the car, connected front and rear by torsion boxes, which provide its structural integrity. To provide for passenger occupation, the rear torsion box incorporates a roll-over structure, the rear of the seat mounting, and a larger section with a sliding joint and the crumple zone where the rear subframe bolts on. At the front is the front of the seat mounting, the top of the steering column mount, where the crash structure goes on.

The original challenge was to produce an efficient chassis structure. Tony Shute drew a comparison between an archaic Austin Seven chassis, with very low stiffness and a very inefficient structure, and at the other extreme a modern Group C sports racer with a carbon tub, which is very light and very stiff. The target was to create a chassis with 10,000Nm per degree stiffness at a weight of about 154lb (70kg). Such a chassis would be some seven times stiffer than a Lotus Seven, or three times stiffer than the Esprit. Research indicated this target was world class for an open top car.

The next decision Lotus had to make was whether to weld or to bond the chassis components, and much research was done into both methods. The bonding-only method indicated that it would absorb very high loads, but once those loads were exceeded the structure had nothing left to rely on. In other words, in an impact situation the joints would tolerate a great deal of stress and then suddenly fall apart. A welded joint, on the other hand, doesn't have a very high peak load, but it does have very good elongation: it doesn't give up like a plain bonded joint. Lotus discovered that the trick is to use a mechanical fastener along with the bonded joint, which not only stops the joint peeling apart, but holds it together during a period of elongation. The Ejot thread-forming fastener is commonly used in the building industry, and these fasteners were selected for the Elise. They were even thought to be so effective that the car could even be driven without bonded joints.

The bond is created by an epoxy adhesive, which doesn't actually cure until the chassis has been into the oven. This meant that the component parts could be disassembled and moved around and adjusted during the experimentation stage. Tony commented:

> They build it in a fixture or jig, and that locates the sections very accurately; then

you put in the Ejot fasteners, which hold it all together before the bond goes off. Once they're in place it's effectively locked together. Then you take it out of the fixture and put it in the oven for four hours.

Lotus designed in extrusion features that don't need a bond at all. Up in the front of the chassis structure the joints lock together through channels in the edges of the extrusions, although in practice they do apply a bond to prevent rattling and to provide a better seal. A great deal of analysis was done on the chassis in order to simulate the offset barrier crash test and to calculate the stiffnesses.

THE STEP-IN CAR

Before the Elise project got under way, a nucleus of senior Lotus Engineering personnel discussed the possibilities of a new model that would revert to the first principles laid down by Colin Chapman. Included in this coterie were former F1 racing driver John Miles, Roger Becker, Ken Sears and Richard Hurdwell. They visualized a step-in car, a car without doors, not dissimilar in concept to a Caterham, which itself was rooted in the Lotus Mark VI and Seven that originated in the mid-1950s, but with 1990s design values. However, the crucial factor was one of access, and it was felt that the concept of window-as-door was not the right way to go, and possibly even more complicated to design – because of weatherproofing requirements – than a conventional door. One reason that the Renault Sport Spider was less effective than the Elise was because its weatherproofing was inadequate. Another, quite different drawback for the Sport Spider was ironically one of

An early rendering done when the project was still at the front-engined 'step-in car' phase – although how you would easily climb aboard is debatable. There were certain similarities with the proposals for the 1998 concept car, the 340R.

Renault's corporate strengths – its multitude of dealerships. While Renault dealerships' expertise lies in selling Clios and Méganes, and lacked dedicated knowledge to market the Spider, Lotus dealerships on the other hand were staffed by specialist sales staff who could focus on the Elise's strengths and provide enthusiast-led sales back-up. This situation is apt to snowball. If the dealer is making money he can employ specialist sales and after-sales staff, and provide better back-up, which in turn is good for the customer.

The other financial aspect is that the Elise proved in its first couple of years to be a sound investment. There was an element of speculation at first, and cars were being sold on at a premium. This was likely to have dried up after four or five years, but bearing in mind the minimal depreciation of the second generation Elan, it looked as if the Elise, with its low running costs, would remain a good investment.

The way in which the team was structured to carry out the project was significant. Tony Shute described the procedure. It went back to the team principle, which was quite difficult to implement for such a complex project. There were minimal levels of management, with responsibility delegated through the organization; the policy was not really to question what people were doing, but to select the right person for each individual job, and then not interfere.

When the Elise project was first mooted, Romano Artioli was very much involved with his Bugatti company, and Lotus was run by Adrian Palmer. The first thing that happened after Mr Artioli took over was that the S2 Elan was put into production, using up stocks of engines and drivetrain componentry. Tony Shute oversaw the engineering of this project as well. A stock of 800 engines was available, and the most practical way to sell these was to turn them into cars, which is effectively what they did. The S2 Elan proved to be very successful, providing unexpected funds

When the Elise project got under way, Romano Artioli was still involved with Bugatti, and Lotus was run by Adrian Palmer. The key personnel here pictured giving it the thumbs up at the Frankfurt launch in 1995 include Richard Rackham, Julian Thomson and Tony Shute at centre, with Artioli on the right. The car's namesake, Artioli's granddaughter, occupies the driver's seat.

that helped finance part of the Elise project. When the stock of Elan S2 engines had dried up – because the factory in Japan had closed down – Lotus Cars would be left with a redundant workforce, so they needed to get the Elise programme going to avoid having to lay off any staff.

It was ironic that the first time around the Elan virtually bankrupted Lotus, while production of the second series made the company a lot of money. At the same time, the Elan and the tooling to make it were being sold to Kia, and this too brought in vital funds.

By 1997, 80 per cent of Group Lotus belonged to the Malaysian-based HiCom Group, who also owned Proton. The Perusahaan OtomoMi Malaysia – or Proton – group took a big step onto the international stage in 1996 by acquiring a majority stake in Lotus, but despite speculation to the contrary based on the downturn in the far eastern economy, in June 1998 the Malaysian parent increased its stake in Group Lotus from 64 to 80 per cent, saying this represented a consolidation of its investment. The extra

16 per cent stake bought by the Proton group was that previously held by former chairman, Tan Sri Yahaya, who invested some of his own cash alongside Proton's to help save Lotus, but who tragically died in a helicopter crash in 1997. The implications of his death may be greater than was at first appreciated, such was his commitment to the Lotus cause. Mr Artioli retained 20 per cent and continued to act for Lotus in the capacity of consultant. Lotus has to remain a viable business just as it did in the General Motors era.

'There's no such thing as free money,' as Tony Shute put it. HiCom Group is there as a backer, and as such it is easier to raise finance for projects. Every new car requires a huge investment to establish the design, development and durability work. And while it was only planned to make a few hundred Elise units a year, that figure had risen to 3,000 a year by 1998, and naturally a great deal more funding was needed to facilitate such a hike. The introduction of a new model is even more demanding of finance because there is a gestation period of two or three years while money is spent

Every car is prepared to delivery standard, which includes being subjected to a water test to check for leaks, and, seen here, a full valet job.

in shovels-full with absolutely no return whatsoever on the investment.

Then as production is increased to, say, three cars a day, the manufacturer has to buy in for four cars a day while still manufacturing three units. This carries on until the rate is ten cars a day, and volume sticks there for some weeks until the buying-in and manufacturing figures tally. Every time the manufacturing figure is increased, the stock situation is made much worse, and this harms the cash flow. There is thus a natural brake on how rapidly the company can expand, and it was important that Lotus Engineering could demonstrate its success to HiCom Group.

Like the Korean manufacturers in the late 1980s, the Malaysians were operating with Japanese-derived technology and styling. Ten years on they were sufficiently mature to want to design and build their own cars, and Lotus Engineering was a logical partner. There is a high degree of security about what Lotus Engineering is actually involved with, but Tony Shute indicated that Lotus are 'helping' Proton with a number of new models. But of

course, they could have received this kind of assistance without going to the trouble of buying Lotus. And despite this they are still not Lotus's biggest customers. Meanwhile, in 1997 the Malaysian economy showed itself to be fragile.

TYPE APPROVAL

The Elise was one of the first cars in the world to have obtained full European vehicle type approval in one go, and the upside of this is that the production process is in control. This is done through process control, by ensuring that all components come within a set of given tolerances before manufacture takes place, rather than merely extracting finished products that are defective. Tony explained:

We homologated the car to European whole vehicle type approval, and passing that is proof that we had process control. We have to show documentation that the processes by which they are made are in control. Not taking one unit and measuring it, which gives a minimum

Regimented rows of components are a rare sight in car plants these days, and such is the efficiency of the Elise production schedule that it's most unusual to see these stacks of front and rear clamshells. Panels are normally made very much on a 'just in time' basis and do not hang around.

sample. Instead you take, say, a hundred units and measure every one, and you show that perhaps twenty are outside the specification. You then make sure those twenty come into specification, and measure another hundred. It's a 100 per cent inspection, and then they're all OK. Out of the next batch of hundred you take twenty, and this establishes that your variation in your process is in control within defined limits, and then you can reduce the sample to one or two. All you

need is documentation to prove that you've been through this process control.

The same is true of components sourced from external suppliers. For example, the silencer maker would have had to ensure that the silencer was manufactured under a controlled process. Furthermore, meeting noise level targets was not achieved by measuring decibels after the car was finished and reacting accordingly, but by incorporating the right kind of silencer into the production process. This means that the whole assembly meets the noise requirements, and this philosophy is true of the construction of the whole car.

Late in 1997 Lotus was involved in matching world-wide quality standards – identified as ISO QS 9000 – which Lotus (and any other supplier) has to meet on behalf of its major clients like Ford and General Motors. They can thus be assured that the build process is under control, right the way from the design function through to manufacturing, including things like the monitoring of inspection gauges.

Supposing a part arrives on the line that doesn't fit – and this does happen occasionally – production control will seek to find out why it could happen, asking whether there was a design malfunction or whether there was a manufacturing fault. The operator's response is important at this point, as there will be a hold-up. He refers to a process that investigates why the problem has arisen. It's an ongoing process and a sophisticated one at that, aimed at continual refinement of the design process. The concept has passed on to General Motors, who produce sixty cars an hour.

Low parts count equals low investment. The tooling for a particular extrusion might be £2,000, against fractions of millions for a pressed steel part. This cost benefit allowed Lotus to design two chassis levels during the pre-prototype phase, and some of the prototype dies were exactly the same as those finally used in production. No additional investment was needed to move into production mode, apart from the fixturing (jigs), required to hold all the components together.

The key to the Elise's project management was the successful integration of the technology partnerships, which involved at least two or three different nations. In terms of the original chassis manufacture it concerned the extrusions division of Hydro Aluminium, Ciba adhesives, and Ejot fasteners. Lotus's expertise lay in predicting the load and stress requirements of the chassis, and its functional needs, such as where the seats fit, and so on.

Components formed from other extrusions included the pedals and pedal boxes, suspension uprights and anti-roll bar brackets. Pedal pads hook around the pedals, making for cost effective assembly. Again, steel pressings would be vastly more expensive.

Brake disc technology started off with the metal-matrix silicon-carbide reinforced aluminium, although at the time of writing (in autumn 1998), Lotus was considering using aluminium oxide as a reinforcement. The aluminium oxide powder is pressed into pre-formed shape, rather like a polystyrene tile, where it contains 70 per cent by volume voids. The lightweight disc thus created is then infused with aluminium alloy, which fills up all the tiny cavities. It is not only strong, but lightweight as well, and capable of running at a further $15°C$ above the silicon-carbide discs – up to $64°C$, in fact. However, its heat conduction is less efficient. It may sound like an exotic technology, but when producing 100,000 discs a year, costs

almost match those of cast iron discs. Tony Shute predicted that alumina drum brakes could be seen within three years.

CRASH STRUCTURE

Tony described some of the more unusual features of the Elise construction. For example, the front crash structure is an RTM composite moulding, based on some research done for a German client. In the event of a frontal impact with something like a tree, the composite crumples progressively in a localized area, absorbing the energy of the impact. It's a little like a concertina effect going down through the structure. Similar cell-constructions are present down the edges to cope with side impacts, and 30mph (50km/h) collisions are easily contained in this way. The structure is designed to be able to withstand 10-ton loads. In the event of such a collision happening, this crash structure can easily be removed and replaced. This member also provides a location for the towing eye and the body mount for the front clamshell, as well as the radiator duct. Like a Group C racer, it's designed to provide front downforce. The unit was actually developed on a steel trolley, and all the barrier tests were carried out independently from the rest of the car.

Another area that is more complicated than perhaps you might imagine is the windscreen surround. This is a one-piece moulding with a foam matrix or armature down the centre. Lotus originally investigated the possibility of making this as a hydroformed tube part, formed by using a steel tube bent into roughly the desired shape, which would then be placed in a die and liquid forced at high pressure up it. This proved to be too expensive, however, and a composite structure was able to carry a greater amount of detail.

The story of the windscreen wiper motor is set to become an industry legend. Interestingly, the screen was designed to meet the requirements of the single wiper. And since the screen defines the height, width and proportions of the entire vehicle, it has a heavy responsibility for the overall concept. As an example of the avenues of research Lotus went down when evolving the Elise, Tony Shute recalled how he visited a French firm that specialized in really complex wiper systems. In detailed discussions with their chief engineer, a slight misunderstanding occurred as to the time scale of the Elise project. When the French engineer realized that it was a four-months project rather than one lasting four years, he declared that it was impossible. Said Tony:

> He asked me, 'how much space have you got to accommodate the wiper?' and I said, 'well, how much do you want – we can design the whole car around it.' But he couldn't cope with that, so I provided a box and he was happy with that. But then he looked at the design for the windscreen, and decided it would be impossible to wipe it. So I said I'd brought a wiper with a bit of Perspex around it that one of our technicians knocked up in the workshop. I produced it and put it on his bench, and they attached a battery to prove it worked. He said, 'this is incredible! Who made this motor?' And I said, 'well, you do!' But they still said it couldn't be done, and didn't want to get involved.

So Lotus found a UK-based specialist to make what they wanted and produce the wiper-motor linkage. Then late in 1997, they received a phone call from the parent company of the specialist that Tony had visited previously. They had seen the Elise wiper mechanism, and now they wanted to buy it from Lotus!

Another aspect of the Elise that was developed in association with a different specialist firm was the instrument panel, and the company concerned was Stack Instruments. This unit is extremely simple, with just one plug lead providing all the functions, and it's also compact and light. By contrast, the more traditional gauges of the Esprit are fed by something approaching a hundred separate wires.

BRAKE MAKERS

The Italian brake specialists Brembo now produce the silicone carbide metal matrix brake discs that were originally designed and made by the Lanxide Corporation in the USA, having acquired the European rights from Lanxide. The Elise uses Koni monotube dampers, which are mounted upside down. Lotus tried to set up the Elise chassis to run without a front anti-roll bar, but the presence of this component shows that it wouldn't work without one.

'We're continually doing detail changes,' said Tony, 'which month by month bring down the build cost slightly.'

The doors are extremely compact units, and contain aluminium beam extrusions, which feature the only aluminium weld in the whole car where the hinge rotor is welded on. This weld is carried out by Hydro Raufoss Automotive at Bromyard, Herefordshire. The Elise thus has two side impact beams, one at the height of the sills, and another a little higher up with the dash cross-beam and the roll-hoop around the back giving it support. The door beam runs right through the length of the door and supports the rest of the window mechanism.

The fact that many of the components

Brembo-made metal matrix compound brake discs are used all round on the SE version, representing a significant weight saving over traditional cast iron discs, as well as better heat dissipation. Magnesium alloy callipers further reduce unsprung weight.

come from different sources is a complication that requires co-ordination, but this is how Lotus have been operating for many years. The purchasing people were part of the Elise project team from day one, as the ability to buy componentry at an affordable price was an essential requirement. 'To design a part that's successful technically is no use if you can't afford it,' said Tony. 'For example, if you design a wishbone that costs £40 when your budget is £10, you've failed.'

The other thing about the chassis is that because it is in a sense modular, Lotus can change 20 per cent of it and create a different car, just by fixing the component parts in different ways. It can be wider, longer or taller, and they can add or delete sections, so it's very cost-effective. A 2+2 can be done, for example, or the engineers can carry out variations to the roof like the one-off Elise spider, with its Lotus 23-style windshield. And the GT1 cars that raced in 1997 were based on a lengthened Elise chassis. Although they were a fresh construction, made during downtime over

weekends at Hydro Aluminium, rather than a cut and shut job, it speaks volumes about the strength of the chassis that they can be adapted for big-time international competition, and could run easily with big 6.0-litre V8 engines.

WEIGHT LOSS

Looking ahead, Lotus also aim to increase the performance of the Elise by further paring down its weight, and are looking at the three-ply windscreen – glass/plastic/glass – considering a two-ply glass and plastic screen instead. The road wheels are relatively unsophisticated low-pressure die-cast, and they could be rolled by the alulite process from a casting. A forging would be too expensive, particularly because it calls for a different size of wheels front and rear. And magnesium would work out at about £200 per wheel, which is too much for a standard car. By weight, tyres are between 30 and 40 per cent steel, so Lotus are looking at lightweight glass-fibre based tyres instead.

The driveshafts are sourced from the Montego Turbo parts bin, and can cope with far more torque than the Rover K-series engine produces; although a relatively humble donor part, they are relatively low cost items, which is the issue here. The gearbox is capable of taking the V6 version, which is way over capacity, but it is also a low-budget item that could otherwise cost Lotus some £10m in pursuing their own lightweight solution. Saving 11lb (5kg) or so doesn't justify such a sum. Another weighty component is the exhaust system, at 48lb (22kg), and a titanium version is being investigated for the 190bhp competition car, which could cost £500. The battery is another aspect where lightweight technology might prove fruitful. Pointing to the diversity of the Elise concept, Tony commented that the 190 Sport competition car was evolving into a sub-10 seconds to 100mph car, which is only just over the Ferrari F40, while at the other end of the scale, the electric Zytec-engined version was a running prototype.

He also mentioned a three-litre (consumption per 100km travelled) version and an 80mpg diesel-powered car as possible side-shoots that were under discussion.

ITALIAN JOBS

The Lotus Elise Trophy was introduced in Italy in 1997, and attracted the interest of many Italian drivers. Peroni Promotions were responsible for all the organization and attracting substantial press and television coverage, as well as paddock hospitality. There were nine races altogether in the 1997 Championship, eight of which were in Italy and one at Rijeka in Croatia. There were two rounds each at Vallelunga, Magione, Misano Adriatico, and Varano. In addition, some Elise Trophy cars raced in the Six Hours of Vallelunga, where the first Elise finished fifth overall. At the Bologna Motor Show, Peroni Promotions organized a demonstration Elise race. There were two half-hour

The Lotus Elise Trophy was introduced in Italy in 1997; entrants used standard road-going Elises fitted with tuning kits supplied by the well-known race preparation firm Conrero.

There were nine races in the 1997 Italian Lotus Elise Championship, with rounds at Vallelunga, Magione, Misano, Varano and Rijeka in Croatia. This is the hectic start at one of the Misano rounds on 11 May.

practice sessions before each race, which was either a single 70km (44-mile) race or two l-hour races.

Nineteen drivers registered for the series, (average age thirty-four), and an average of fifteen cars participated in each race. Drivers with a grade C CSAI licence could register, using a standard Elise fitted with a tuning kit supplied by the long-standing race preparation and tuning firm Conrero. The specification also included

standard wheels shod with Avon tyres, with a weight limit of 760kg (1,672lb) including driver. As part of the deal, drivers also received fire-resistant overalls and undergarments, paddock waistcoats and quilted jackets.

THE MOTORSPORT CAR

In March 1997 Lotus announced the Sport Elise – what the factory refers to as the 190 Motorsport car. It was a logical evolution of the original model and successfully combined the performance and sensation of a competition car with the usability of a road car. The idea – which I thoroughly identify with – was that it could be driven to the circuit and back and used quite happily in any racing discipline without the need for massive sponsorship budgets. I did the same myself with an Alfa Romeo a few years ago, and it was a far better car on the road as a result. To reduce weight as much as possible the Sport 190 can have carbon-fibre clamshells, magnesium wheels, lightweight battery, silencer and rear window glass, bringing its weight

The Elise Sport (or 190 Motorsport model, as it was known in house) can be fitted with carbon-fibre clamshells – like this pair awaiting paint – and they are as much as fifty per cent lighter than GFRP (glass-fibre reinforced plastic).

Tony Shute drove the factory's 190 Motorsport car at the Prescott hillclimb, where he was 1.5 seconds quicker than the 200bhp Caterhams – and in the wet too, which said much for the Elise's superior traction.

down to 1,430lb (650kg). Options include an FIA-approved roll cage, a full four-point harness, competition springs, dampers, anti-roll bar, competition Stack instrument pack with data-logging facility, a closer ratio gearbox and competition silencers. A tonneau cover was a sensible option.

The Sprint 190 Motorsport car was tested at Prescott hillclimb and the Brighton speed trials in 1997 and attracted seventy-five orders before the year's end, which Tony viewed with some incredulity. 'Who'd have thought we could sell that many Elises at £34,000?' he wondered. I reflected that Caterham's special edition Jonathan Palmer JPE model was listed at

that sort of money, and Caterham race cars probably cost as much to develop.

It's early days as far as the Elise's competition programme is concerned, but already the signs are good. At Prescott, Tony Shute was 1.5 seconds quicker than the 200bhp Caterhams in the wet. 'The Elise is pretty quick – and good in the wet,' he said, 'but you have to be careful. The Caterhams are about 500kg [1,100lb], while the Elise is nearer 700 [1,540lb], so we're actually down on power to weight, but the Elise clearly has better traction.'

The initial batch of motorsport cars was built up in one off the workshops off the production line because of the difficulties of installing special components and interfering with the tight schedule on the line. The optional carbon-fibre clamshells were actually made by ex-Lotus F1 crewman Arthur Birchill, and could have a paint finish that would show off the material. Several of the cars were destined for Australia and the USA to compete against 911s and the like in the Bathurst sports car event, and the cars were fitted with the hard-tops that are mandatory in Australia. The Australian importer is Andrew Smith, and the operation is financed by Dean Wills, chairman of Coca-Cola there, and who had just built a 3-mile (5km) test track in his back garden.

MARKET POTENTIAL

Lotus are mindful of what attracts a lot of customers to their opposition. For example, Caterham buyers are often people who have always wanted a Seven, and get one when they come into money. It may be a second car, and they may hang on to it forever, or sell after a year when they've proved their point. It is not yet absolutely clear what attracts someone to Elise ownership. Clearly the looks and the driving experience have a lot to do with it. At the Lotus 50th Anniversary celebrations in September 1998, the PR team reckoned that almost half the 1,500 or so Lotuses that arrived from all over the world were Elises. That could suggest that there is a new breed of Lotus enthusiast who is buying the Elise. I was present on the day of the party, and the sight of so many Lotuses of one sort or another and the number of visitors present was most heartening. Even when the heavens opened, people's enthusiasm was not dampened, and with Hazel Chapman and Lotus managing director Chris Knight cutting the 'birthday' cake in the huge marquee, it seemed to augur well for the future.

Tony Shute was surprised that there were still speculators in the market for the Elise two years after the car had been in production, but then they're still around at Morgan, taking advantage of the seven-year waiting list. Tony pondered whether Morgans are bought by young people, or whether they are only sought by a generation that will inevitably die out one day. No doubt there will always be a steady trickle of customers world-wide, and indeed, one day Charles Morgan may even bring the car's underlying structure into the twenty-first century.

Like TVR, Lotus are diffident about selling in the USA because of the potentially ruinous product liability laws; in addition, the process of federalizing the Elise makes it even less desirable in the land where biggest is still best. A small, lightweight car with a frugal engine that costs about the same as a Porsche Boxster and not much less than a Corvette is at something of a disadvantage in the States. As well as adding weight and slowing the car down, the federalizing process possibly requires airbags. Adding more power to overcome the deficit simply raises the price, and Lotus are not sure the investment is worth it.

As I was just finishing the book something came up by way of a postscript. Journalists from *Autocar* magazine suggested to Lotus that they might like to consider a more radical version of the Elise, and taking a written-off chassis as a basis, the in-house design team set about making a prototype. It was to be a much more futuristic vehicle, a rotund wedge shape with lots of scoops, louvres and slashes, yet displaying some traditional cues like Caterham-style cycle-wing mudguards.

The Elise may be a lightweight, but it was planned to extract a further 440lb (200kg) by abandoning such creature comforts as doors, side windows and heater system. It would use the 170bhp version of the K-series engine, coupled to a close ratio gearbox, and the power-to-weight ratio would match that of the 911 Turbo. That would be 340bhp per ton, which provided a working title for the car – the 340R. It was launched in October 1998 at the NEC motor show.

Development of the Rover K-Series Engine

The K-series engine was first conceived as far back as 1984, and according to Rover Group's Bickenhill-based project manager, John Gibbs, it had already become clear to Rover what the development of a competitive range of power units would entail: 'It would mean radically lower emission levels, coupled with high performance and fuel economy.' Nothing too surprising there, but nevertheless these requirements called for a very advanced engine, clean burning, yet capable of much higher specific power. At the same time it had to be highly reliable, and cheap to use and run. So although the goals were fairly obvious, achieving them involved something of a quantum leap.

A number of alternatives were considered. Developing the company's almost prehistoric A-series engine family to achieve the radical changes necessary would require an overhead camshaft working bigger valves. This would in turn need wider cylinder bore spacing – in effect the development of a substantially new engine accompanied by the huge expense of a new engine line. At the end of the day it would still be an A-series motor, and would therefore carry weight and design limitations.

Rover looked at other engines available in the market-place that they could buy or invest in on a joint venture basis. The initial range of possibilities seemed wide, but the options were progressively eliminated because of production limitations, or because designs didn't provide the right sort of development potential. It was therefore decided to design a completely new engine in house.

Work on the three-cylinder, twelve-valve ECV3 project at the company's research and testing centre at Gaydon had already given some early leads in low emission, multi-valve, lightweight engine technology.

Initially, three concept engines were developed – four-cylinder units in 1.3- and 1.1-litre capacities, and a three-cylinder 1.0-litre. However, a combination of concerns over refinement, and the move towards 1.4-litres as one of the proposed European emission level boundaries, plus the certainty that performance standards would increase, made the design team opt for a four-cylinder family of engines of 1.1 and 1.4 litres. This was to become the K-series. A four-valve combustion chamber would be designed for the most powerful 1.4-litre K16, with the remainder in two-valve K8 form. Other derivatives, such as the 1.8-litre unit we are concerned with in the Elise, would come later.

Four-valve combustion chambers in a British family car engine was an exotic concept in 1984, but this arrangement had even then been shown to offer the most certain route to the cleanest combustion, while preserving high specific power. This was particularly the case when allied to lean-burn part-throttle running – in which Rover has been among the leaders in research and production. The M16 engine in the Rover 800 series is a good example. After a great deal of emissions and endurance testing, two fuel systems were selected. These were the KIF constant velocity carburettor and an electronically controlled throttle body single-point injection system for the K16 version.

Cast iron has traditionally been the favoured material for the cylinder block of most production engines, but it always had the drawback of heavy weight. Modern steel engines like the Fiat-derived Alfa Romeo TwinSpark motor have to a degree transcended that. However, silicon alloys of aluminium weigh, for the same volume, roughly two-thirds less – though for an application like a cylinder block, some of this weight advantage is lost in providing extra metal thickness to counter the strength deficiencies of such light alloys. According to John Gibbs, Rover engineers considered a wide variety of designs for an all aluminium-alloy-cased engine that made the most of the advantages of light alloys, and that could be produced at the lowest cost. As a result, the advanced construction principle of the K-series was born.

The engine case – meaning the cylinder head, block and crankcase – of the K-series unit consists of four aluminium alloy castings. Starting at the top, under the die-cast camshaft cover, there is a ladder-like casting, the rungs of which are the upper halves of the two sets of six camshaft bearings. The lower halves are formed in the top of the cylinder head, casting number two. The cylinder block, carrying the cylinder liners, forms the main casting, ending on the crankshaft centre line.

Instead of fixing the crankshaft in place with separate main bearing caps bolted to the underside of the block, the K-series borrows from racing engine practice. Thus, it uses a deep-sided bottom casting, another ladder like the cam-bearing one above, but considerably larger, and closed by the sump, which is a conventional steel pressing. Die-cast LM24 specification is used for the two bearing ladders and Rover's own low-pressure sand casting technique for the block and head in heat-treated LM25. All castings are located by dowels. When bolted in place, the combination of the main bearing ladder and the block gives every K-series engine an immensely stiff bottom end. This means that the engine can safely exploit higher crankshaft speeds, vibration is reduced, there is better support for the main bearings, and, because the engine is deeper and stiffer in all planes, it can be made lighter.

Through-Bolt Construction

The method of bolting together the castings of K-series motor presented another opportunity for developing a significantly different design. Conventionally the camshaft-bearing ladder is bolted to the head, and the head and main bearing ladder are each bolted to the block, each joint secured by its own set of bolts. Rover perceived that if these bolts could be in line with each other, the two sets could be replaced by a single set of long ones.

This concept was first applied on the prototype 1.3-litre K-series that first ran on 6 July 1985. It used ten very long (412mm x 9mm diameter) specially made steel bolts, tying the casting together between their forged heads and, at the lower end, specially rolled threads screwed into the tree-like die-casting. This combined the functions of a clamping nut-plate for the bolts, and an oil gallery for the main bearings. The K-series' long through-bolts expand much less readily than the engine's aluminium alloy, so they are tightened less severely than usual on assembly, the design clamping load only being developed after the first time the engine achieves its normal running temperature. The slenderness of the bolts ensures that they have more than enough 'spring' to minimize changes in dynamic stress in them.

Aluminium alloy is least strong when subjected to tension. But in the K-series block assembly, it's the through-bolts that take all tension loads caused by the pressure pulses of the working and other strokes from cylinder head to main bearings. That allows the block and head assembly to be lighter, as no allowance has to be made for tensile loads in the castings. In a conventional engine, cylinder bores can be easily distorted as head-bolts are tightened. This is not the case with the K-series' through-bolts. Their symmetrical distribution helps avoid the distortion that aluminium engines can be prone to, by spreading the clamping load evenly.

In that first 1985 engine each bolt was placed down the outside of the block between each cylinder, exposed to view. It didn't stay like that though, and Rover quickly took the decision to encapsulate the bolts to eliminate the risk of potential oil leaks, and improve the general appearance of the unit. Covering up the bolts where they ran outside the block is one reason why the K-series is an unusually tidy engine, with few external hoses. The cast-in covers form vertical passageways down the sides of the head, block and main openings to the camshaft and crankshaft spaces. These provide very good crankcase ventilation ducts and also passages through which oil could return to the sump without first hitting the rotating crankshaft. This reduces oil dispersion and, more usefully, some of the energy-wasting drag on the crank. The through-bolt system does impose some special needs, however, and additional short bolts keep the main bearing ladder in place if the through-bolts are removed for any reason.

Rotating Parts

The solid graphite cast-iron crankshaft has five 45mm-diameter main bearings, carried in indium-flashed aluminium-tin bearing shells with 43mm crank pins, and is fully counterweighted for optimum balance. Clutch thrust loads are carried via the centre main bearing. There is a multi-lobe type oil pump on the crankshaft nose, with an integral pressure-relief valve venting into the pump inlet, another measure that minimizes oil aeration. Cast-in and drilled oil-ways avoid the need for any external oil hoses. All engine sizes share the same size flywheel, complete with reluctor ring for engine speed and piston position signalling to the electronic engine management unit.

Heat-treated drop-forged steel connecting rods have 18mm gudgeon pins and are 131.5mm between centres; this comparatively generous length is made possible by increasing the overall height of the engine by 14mm from that used in the original 1,300cc unit, to preserve the same standard of secondary out-of-balance forces. Pistons are strutted internally, and have three rings.

A 25mm-wide toothed belt proven to over 100,000 miles (160,000km) drives chilled cast-iron camshafts. With the cam drive cover removed, the considerably lightened camshaft pulley wheels

A K-series engine nears the end of the line at Rover's Longbridge plant. With the cam drive cover yet to be fitted the camshaft pulley wheels are prominent, and the semi-automatic tensioned belt also drives the water pump.

are visible. The ignition distributor is neatly mounted on one end of the inlet camshaft. The belt also drives the water pump and has a semi-automatic sprung belt tensioner – thus diminishing manual setting of the tensioner in production. The wet cylinder liners are in centrifugal cast iron, and each one is located in the top of the cylinder block. They are spaced 88mm apart, and supported laterally at their lower ends, which are sealed with two O rings.

Casting inaccuracies can impair fluid flow around the cylinders of a traditional bored cast block, but in the K-series the combination of a low pressure sand-cast block and wet liners ensures coolant spaces of consistent size, which can therefore be smaller. These are fed and exhausted in a crossflow manner from coolant distribution channels along each side of the block-head joint, which is in turn fed by the integral water pump driven by the timing drive. Because it is guided and pumped precisely, the overall volume of coolant is very low – just 1.2 litres – guaranteeing a rapid warm-up from cold. The gasket that makes the seal between head and block is a stainless steel backbone type, with flame rings making the compression joint between liner and head and a moulded elastomeric bead for fluid sealing.

Cylinder Head

All K-series engines use hydraulic tappets rated to a maximum of 7,200rpm, and this is a major reason why the K-series is a low maintenance engine, with no need for valve clearance adjustment. The K16 has 28mm inlet valves and 24mm exhausts, set almost symmetrically at an included angle of 45 degrees, with separate inlet and exhaust camshafts providing 8.2mm of lift into a normal pent-roof combustion chamber with a central l4mm threaded sparking plug. Single valve springs are fitted. A lot of work went into evolving cam profiles, which minimized noise whilst preserving performance. Cast channels in the joint face between head and cam carrier provide oil-ways for the tappets and valve gear.

The four-valve combustion chamber was originally designed to make the most of a careful balance between swirl and volumetric efficiency to provide the fast burn rates needed to allow very lean mixtures. The swirl principle is similar to that used in the award-winning M16 engine in the Rover 800 series. Mixture entering through the inlet valves gives a broadly circular swirling motion about a horizontal line – barrel swirl – to the chamber contents. As the piston rises, the barrel is made smaller in diameter, which forces a higher rate of rotation.

Near top-dead-centre the space becomes too cramped for swirl to continue, but it still has a lot of energy which it dissipates in 'micro-swirl' – hundreds of tiny turbulences that are ideal for very rapid combustion. The compactness of the pent chamber and the closeness of the central spark plug combine to produce very good conditions for fast burn, which is essential for the thorough combustion of very lean mixtures. Cyclic variations in mixture strength are much more tightly controlled in the K16 chamber, particularly at or near idle, where lean burn combustion makes a further contribution to a cleaner engine. After all, one of the most important design aims of the K-series was that it should be capable of meeting any emissions limit likely to be imposed in the foreseeable future.

The electronically controlled throttle body single point injection system on a K16 engine is a Rover Group development, which uses a Bosch-supplied injector, and the familiar PTC (Positive Temperature Coefficient) electric mixture heater on a special tuned-length inlet manifold. An electronic engine management unit (MEMS, or Modular Engine Management System) controls the fuel and ignition systems. This was one of the early fruits of Rover's own Gaydon-based electronic hardware and software design facility. Rover now design and develop their own electronic engine management hardware and software in conjunction with Motorola at Hitchin, Hertfordshire.

MEMS is based around an Intel 8096 microprocessor. It has an eight-kilobyte memory, using surface mount methods for automatic assembly and to reduce the size of the control unit, and it allows full diagnostics using Rover's own ROSCO (ROver Service COmmunications protocol), which is common to all Rover products and service test equipment. Plug-in modules allow expansion to full US 83 closed-loop emission control when required. In its control of the throttle body injection it relies on speed density air flow measurement rather than any form of air meter.

The Champion spark plug used in K-series engines is a double copper type, in which both the centre and earth electrodes are copper-cored for better heat transfer. The conventional nickel alloy, copper-cored, earth electrode is trapezoidal in section, presenting a 50 per cent wider area to the spark, thus giving less erosion and longer life. The plug is also more resistant to cold fouling, and reduces risk of pre-ignition.

Durability Testing

Perhaps unsurprisingly, the K-series engine is the most thoroughly tested power unit that Rover have ever developed. Durability testing covered just less than two million miles (3 million km), plus 73,000 hours of specific high and low speed testing. In its infancy, no fewer than seventy-two K-series engined Montegos ran in the hands of closely monitored non-expert drivers. In Rover's validation programme, the K-series motors were habitually run to 800 hours (100,000 miles or 160,000km) which was twice the previous standard. A total of 875 prototype engines were built during its development.

Many features of the K-series – like hydraulic tappets that never need adjusting, electronic engine management system and camshaft drive belt – contribute to eliminating areas of conventional servicing. Main service intervals conform to Rover's usual 12,000 miles (19,000km) for oil and filter change, but routine service times are reduced by 60 per cent compared with comparable engine types over a 48,000-mile (77,000km) or four-year period.

The K-series engine and R65 gearbox are built at Longbridge in what was in the late 1980s a

Rover's K-series engines are built at Longbridge on a mixture of manual, flexible and dedicated assembly lines. The aluminium cylinder block carries the liners and forms the main casting, ending on the crankshaft centre line, here inverted on a jig and ready for the assembly process to begin.

new £200m state-of-the-art manufacturing facility. Much of the investment was in advanced manufacturing systems, using a mix of manual, flexible and dedicated assembly lines, which ensured high productivity and quality levels, and provided flexibility for future model changes. The new facilities included two new primary metal processing plants that reduced the amount of subsequent machining needed, low-pressure sand casting for the major aluminium parts and precision metal forming for gears.

The R65 gearbox is manufactured at Longbridge in the Cofton Hackett factory, specially refurbished and equipped at a cost of £75 million with an assortment of flexible, manual and dedicated assembly equipment. That includes over a hundred circular robots, and six large gantry robots. The plant has three transfer lines for machining operations: gearbox casing, first stage machining of clutch cases, and second stage machining of finished bores. As with K-series engine production, gear manufacture makes use of new primary metal processes, and in this case, it's precision metal forming (PMF), a technique used to produce blanks for all seven gears used in the gearbox.

By the time it's completed each K-series engine has undergone more than 300 individual checks and measurements. What Rover call 'statistical process control techniques' are used, based on extensive in-cycle and in-process gauging, with the emphasis on preventing faults rather than detecting them later.

In the machining processes, new tool-management techniques have been introduced to boost plant availability. All machines have in-built diagnostics, including tool-wear monitoring, ensuring that tools are replaced as soon as significant wear is detected. Extensive use of automated mechanical handling systems contributes to plant efficiency and product quality. For instance, in the gearbox assembly plant a 2-mile (3.5km) long platen highway moves components from station to station in order to prevent damage.

Chronology of the Rover Contract

Before the Elise project even got under way, Lotus were in discussion with Rover about low-weight vehicle research, and one of the projects under consideration was a sports car that would highlight Lotus technology. It was agreed that the K-series engine was the lightest power unit that was suitable for such a car. After some exchanges of information, Hugh Kemp and Tony Shute made a preliminary visit to Rover HQ on 8 July 1994.

Heading Rover's Power Train Business Development was John Gibbs, and he formed a core team within the company, consisting of Dave Field, Power Train External Projects, and Tony Shipway, International Purchase Collaboration. Following a number of visits and discussions, a strategy meeting was held in Hethel on 13 September 1994. Here they established the ground rules in terms of the performance and functional requirements of the engine and car, the detailed engine installation, what parts Rover would supply and how the deal would be struck.

They agreed that Rover would supply Lotus with its complete 1.8 K-series/PG1 powertrain, including electronics and engine and gearbox mounting systems. In addition, Lotus would buy some other items from Rover to reduce development and component costs. Key performance parameters were established, including a goal of a 0–100km/h (0–60mph) time of less than 6 seconds.

Those present at the meeting included the Rover Core Team of Gibbs, Field and Shipway, and representing Lotus, Tony Shute, John Walker and Richard Rackham. They established an extremely good rapport, which set the tone for a very successful collaboration. Regular joint meetings were held subsequently, at which the details of the programme were developed.

Two key points were clarified during this period. The 0–100km/h target was achieved by computer prediction, bettered in fact at 5.5secs. Initially Tony Shute was not really enthusiastic about using the base 1.8 K-series engine, even though it had apparently achieved the target acceleration time. According to John Gibbs, what he really wanted was the VVC engine, but it was too early for Rover to sell it to another company because of capacity restrictions:

> We often teased him about that. As experience was gradually gained with the engine, performance improvements were made, though. I gained approval from MGF product director Nick Fell that we could use the MGF power unit installation in the Elise, and allayed his fears that the car would be a direct competitor.

The most significant milestone reached in this period was the development of the M1-11 buck, and the time an engine was run in that buck was on 24 December 1994. Thereafter the project became business as usual for Rover, as more people were co-opted on to the programme and much of the detail for the power unit and component supply programme was developed. Purchasing responsibility at Lotus was now in the hands of Nigel Harrington, who developed the contract arrangement through John Gibbs.

When Lotus completed testing of one of the fully engineered prototypes at Nardo in August 1995, Rover's Neil Butler was present. He had taken over from Dave Field as the Rover Engineering project leader. The Rover team brought more staff into the programme in support of the production of the Elise and the after-sales side, and proposed to Hugh Kemp that they should run a series of team development events to promote inter-company bonding. Consultants Thomas Owen & Klove were hired to develop a programme. The first such event took place in mid-January 1996 at Hagley, Worcestershire, and was very successful. Said John Gibbs: 'The final group exercise gave everyone a real buzz, when we achieved the target, which involved engineering a miniature roller coaster ride.'

Follow-up team events were held at Hethel and Rover HQ in the next couple of months. The engineering sign-off was held at Hethel on 21 May 1996. Contract negotiations were concluded, and Hugh Kemp and Alex Stephenson, managing director of Rover Power Train, signed the supply contract on 16 July 1996.

The Elise Sport model features the 135bhp Lotus Sport 16-valve version of the K-series twin cam engine.

2 Factory Tour

Lotus's manufacturing engineering manager Luke Bennett joined the company in 1990 as a manufacturing engineer, and he gave me a thorough tour of the factory. He began:

> We design cars and turn them into something we can actually manufacture. I look after a team of twelve people who liaise with our engineering designers, and our shop floor staff. They communicate between the two, so if there is a change that needs to be made onto the car, maybe something simple, or legislative, or maybe a change for improvement and design, we interpret that and actually break a change on the line.

You get the impression that this is the bottom line, the place where the buck actually stops. Luke and his colleagues are also responsible for buying jigs and fixtures, and working out how long things take to build. It is they who establish the standard time scales that it will take to make things; they establish best operating practices.

'Generally speaking, anything that goes on in the factory, we will have input into it,' said Luke. 'That is what we do as manufacturing engineers. I also look after the tool room, where we manufacture our mould tools, and there are twenty of us in there. We predominantly make Lotus tools, but we also make tools for our clients.'

At this point, Lotus were manufacturing fifty-seven units of the Elise a week, as well as seven Esprits, and could sell just as many as it could make. The company was looking for opportunities to increase that, maybe by extending the working week or introducing alternative methods to try to make a few more. The Proton factory has all the facilities to manufacture the Elise in Malaysia but in mid-1998 nothing had been built:

Manufacturing manager Morris Dowton, left, has worked at Lotus for thirty-three years – since the Cheshunt days in fact – and views the Elise very much as a car in the Chapman mould. Here he discusses manufacturing performance with assembly supervisor Jon Peeke-Vout, who reports regularly to Morris on product quality by vehicle.

Because of economic conditions, they are trying to understand what their market-place is again. And obviously their main lifeblood is making Protons so that is what they are focusing on right now. Of course they are buying kits from us while the pound is very strong and their own currency is relatively weak.

QUALITY STANDARDS

There are numerous work stations in the Lotus plant, and some are manufacturing components in small batches that they supply to the assembly line, and some shops are actually in the manufacturing process. It

is a fairly slow procedure – the flow line – to reach the mainstream body manufacture. Other shops will be supplying smaller parts, like brackets that are made in batches, and which are not on the flow line. First port of call on our tour was the area where the team from the engineering shop meets once a day to discuss quality issues. They are governed by Quality Standard 9000, which is a motor industry version of ISO 9000. Said Luke: 'We are a little bit special, in as much as we employ QS 9000 across all of our engineering and manufacturing operations, which is currently unique in the UK.'

This QS 9000 is a quality system prescribed by the big three: Ford, General Motors and Chrysler. They are very

Engineering manager Luke Bennett (left) explains the significance of the visual information boards prominent in the body manufacturing process to the author. They are among the simplest of management devices, and list all the mould tools, and with a simple traffic light system indicating their status. Red means something requires attention, yellow shows that planned maintenance is pending, and green says there is no problem – tool operable.

prescriptive about what they expect their consultancies and suppliers to be able to do in terms of manufacturing controls, and once a company is certified as QS 9000 approved, it is subjected to a regular series of audits.

BOARD MEETINGS

The engineering team leaders and process control operators who measure the viscosity of the resin meet by the QS board charts every day at 4.00pm with the men from the shop floor to discuss the issues of the day. These meetings cover any quality concerns, production targets, and equipment problems. The object is to control the daily manufacturing operation, and the board on the wall (there is a similar one in every workshop) monitors day-to-day performance, providing operators with ten measures of Lotus's performance in business. For example, it indicates current quality levels measured by their quality assurance department; how much per hour it costs to build the cars, and whether they were on target, or whether any materials were damaged in the manufacturing process. These boards were one of the requirements for obtaining the QS 9000 certificate. Luke explained:

> It's an example of Japanese-style visual quality management, where the operator can see at a glance the state of his operation. We were employed by General Motors from the early 1980s into the 90s, and they put a lot of emphasis on continuous improvement technology, where you aim to keep improving your process all the time. It amounts to a lot of team work, driven from the top, and the results impressed a lot of people.

The technical specifications for each of the mould tools tell the operators (almost like a training manual) the kind of gel flow, the type of matting, how many shots of resin to manufacture a particular component, and so on – and there's one for every component they make. This is in spite of the fact that once an operator has been at Lotus for three to six months, he will have become fully skilled anyway.

Another board identifies all the operators and the size and nature of the tasks they perform. Certain codes indicate which one is qualified to do a particular job, or can do the job but needs to be supervised, or is under training. This is another QS 9000 requirement, and helps pinpoint the kind of skills available at Lotus and what type of training they need to carry out in the future.

A lot of chemicals are used in a car plant like Lotus, and you can smell them too in some places. Accordingly there are a number of notice boards with information referring to the control of hazardous chemicals. Others carry the basic data for running the factory such as the temperature and humidity, which affects the rate at which the resin goes off, so clearly this has to be measured every day.

Yet another board provides the status on the mould tools. It is a very simple traffic light system; if a particular tag is turned over from green to amber or red it means that there is a problem, for instance that there is something amiss with headlight bevels. A maintenance crew that works a late shift cures these sorts of hiccups.

There are some unexpected safety aspects. Luke pointed out an air-driven motor, used instead of an electric one because of the chemical fumes. In the offices where the ceilings are lower, all the light fittings are intrinsically safe to preclude any wayward sparks.

I indicated a small booklet hanging on a red post and Luke told me it was an

Operators are totally responsible for product quality, and carry out a final inspection at the end of the assembly line. Here Paul Clark checks the build manual; any one of the operators can fulfil this role.

instruction book for building the car, belonging to someone working on the line. The book states which parts to use, the sequence of assembly, and torque settings. Further instructions cover the 'move-up' times, stating how long a particular build stage takes before the car must be moved to its next stage. 'For instance, it's exactly thirty-eight minutes to this work station,' said Luke. 'That's the difference between fifty-five cars a week and sixty.'

ON THE MAT

The Elise body parts start life at the fibreglass matting department, where the operators select the raw materials, glass fibres and resins. Lotus source their mats from an Italian company called Vetrotex. It's a bit like a carpet shop or draper's. There are rolls of matting of different thickness and textures hanging up and stacked in piles. Templates also hang conveniently by, while white-coated

Operators select the appropriate matting for the Elise, and cut it into patterns for hand-laying and the VARI process.

operators cut the sheets to pre-ordained sizes and shapes.

The number of sheets they cut is restricted by what you could push a knife through. They use templates in much the same way as a tailor cutting suit material or a shoemaker cutting leather for shoes, and they lay them out so as to incur the minimum amount of waste. And the next time they cut a particular mat it might be a completely different configuration.

There are plenty of general glass-fibre mats of the sort that you might expect to see, and some of the more unusual weavings that give the matting extra strength in areas like the seat mountings or where the body is bolted to chassis. Luke was at pains to assure me of its robustness:

> We have a stitch mat, which is very, very strong but is also very stable. Glass-fibre is notorious for rippling in its curing process; so if you've got a broad, flat panel, you put this type of mat in and it stabilizes the panel. We also use a type of honeycomb, which actually spaces two layers of glass fibre to make a stronger structure. And an Elise has this complete range of mats – apart from the Kevlar, which is used in the Esprit. So there are about twenty different types of matting, all told.

The matting comes from Italy because this is one of the few European countries that actually produce it. It is obtainable from Owens in the USA, but Vetrotex is the nearest and probably the most commercially effective company that Lotus could find. They enjoy a good relationship, to the extent that when an operator on the line at Lotus perceived a problem with some matting, Vetrotex flew him over to Italy and they sorted out the quality problem on the spot.

The number on each template tells the operator what it's to be used for. For instance, number 31 is for six layers of $450g/m^2$ of continuous filament mat, or CFM. It's constructed rather like a jumper if you pull a thread – it will just keep going and going. The opposite of this is chop strand mat, which is made up of little fibres. This type of mat is used for hand laminating processes, without using a bucket and brush, and it is moulded by hand. As the operator works it, it breaks down and can be pushed into all the nooks and crannies. The continuous filament mat is the stronger of the two because it has longer chains of fibre, and it is used in the VARI process (vacuum-assisted resin injection), which, because it takes place in a closed mould, will push that mat into all the complex shapes. So the operators don't have to work hard at it.

GETTING LAID UP

Once the matting has been laid up in the VARI mould, the next stage is injecting the resin into the mould socket. The operator flows the resin into the funnel, allowing it to overfill (so that no air can get in), and then he fits a plug that closes the mould. The vacuum is thus maintained.

The windscreen surround is particularly complex, as it has to be a structural member of the car. The glass-fibre is wrapped around the foam, and placed in a mould with other mats. The mould is closed, and a complete moulding comes out of a single application. Pieces of polyurethane plastic are also moulded in, which will serve to pick up screws later in the process. This is the kind of benefit derived from sophisticated glass-fibre technology – a windscreen surround made out of steel would probably be made up of ten pieces spot-welded together.

When creating any type of mould, the engineers first have to make a pattern, and

After the vacuum is applied to the VARI tool, the resin is injected into the mould. The white plug shows where the injection point is. The gun shown here mixes and catalyses the resin as it is injected.

This moulding demonstrates the technical complexity possible with the VARI process. Here, the mould tool is being loaded prior to being closed. It includes the foam beams, glass-fibre and polyurethane inserts to make a complete Elise windscreen surround. The foam beam provides a core, with glass fibre surrounding it to form a structure.

of course with the Elise they were starting from scratch. In this case the patterns were made from a material called uriol, and a model was carved out of this in order to assess its mouldability. The engineers needed to be certain there would be no situations producing die lock, which is where male and female members won't interlock.

The first application in the mould is the pink gel coat, which is the surface that will be painted, and it's there to give a really smooth surface on the panel for the paint to go on to. If there wasn't a gel coat, the glass-fibre would have an almost porous surface that would require an enormous amount of work to bring up to a flawless finish. After the gel coat – about 1mm thick – there's a 2mm thickness of woven matting in two layers, making an average overall panel depth of about 3mm. But because it's being laid up by hand it's not absolutely consistent. The hand-laid process is the

Lou – the only female operator on the body moulding shop – is hand laminating an Elise front clamshell. She is suitably protected with goggle glasses and rubber gloves.

All hand-laminated components are cured at 60°C for four hours and a further 24 hours at ambient temperature, which is the stage these front clamshells have reached.

method that involves the chopped strand mats, which the operators lay up using hand rollers and brushes. The higher the glass to resin ratio the better, because this makes the matting stronger and less likely to cause any problems downstream.

With this moulding process it is very important that the components are allowed to cure properly, which explains why quite a few components can be standing curing at any one time. From the moulding the panels go into a large oven for five to six hours at 60°C. They're then allowed to stand for 24 hours without any stress being put on them, and then they're baked once more in the next process downstream at 80°C for an hour. This seemingly convoluted process is necessary so that they do not cure too quickly. If the panels cure too fast they tend to buckle and distort, and bubbles of distortion cause trouble at the painting stage.

The beauty of this rather labour

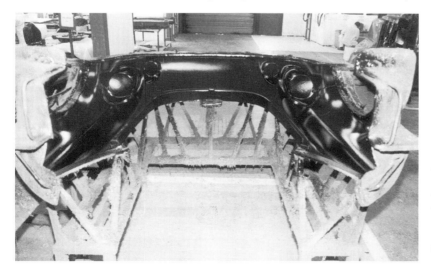

The front clamshell mould tools are made up of six segments that are fastened together. This method enables a complete front-end moulding to be manufactured in one shot. This one has already been gel-coated and is ready to be hand laminated.

The cycle time of the clamshell mouldings means that there are nine tool sets in rotation. This is a technically challenging mould to laminate, and the operator is trained for at least two weeks in the job before being allowed to manufacture production parts.

At the other end of the scale, some parts of the Elise structure are very simple to design and manufacture.

intensive process is that a complete front end emerges from a single mould. Luke pointed out that if it were to be made with a closed mould process like the VARI system, it would have to be joined up from all the pieces where flash lines were evident. As it is, on the front clamshell there are eight segments and on the rear clamshell there are twelve pieces to the mould. They are all bolted together with their individual sections in place, and when they are unbolted, one complete moulding pops out. Lotus moulds its own one-piece bucket seats as well. The disadvantage of the hand-laying method is that it is quite labour intensive, and Lotus has nine sets of tools to manufacture its current production volume. So of the nine rear and nine front mould tools which are in use at any one time, seven are in the manufacturing process and two are being cleaned and prepared for the next day. This works on a cyclical basis, so that during the course of a week all the mould tools will be rid of their build-up of waxes and styrene, which is a legacy of the curing process.

The rear clamshells are manufactured in the same way as the fronts, although the rear one is composed of eleven segments. The tool thus comprises eleven sections that are fastened together and laid up as a whole.

VARI TECHNICAL

We move on into the more technical, more up-market VARI process here. Both Esprit and Elan moulds are still present here, and among the Elise panels made by this method is the sill side moulding, which is quite a complicated moulding. It contains the door aperture, and the technique for making it in one piece is very important in that doors are traditionally very difficult to manufacture, and accuracy is critical. Luke explained:

Whatever those tolerances are, they all want to escape into the door hole, and it is very important that you control that as accurately as you can; that was the principle of making the side sill moulding in one piece. It is also made out of a resin that we call low-profile, which is actually filled with something called milicarb, which is like milled glass and chalk, and it actually displaces the resin. There's one part to every three of resin. One advantage is that milled glass and chalk is cheaper

General view of the VARI moulding area – during a tea break – showing moulds and hoists.

Some mouldings, like the Elise hard-top seen here, are formed by the VARI method, and are locked together using clamping systems like this.

than resin in the first place but its biggest benefits are that it stabilizes the resin so it is much less prone to distortion under heat, and it has a far faster curing cycle.

Lotus only have one mould tool for this panel, rather than the nine in the hand-laying shop, but it can complete its cycle every forty minutes because the curing can be accelerated by applying hot water at 100°C around the mould tool. About half a millimetre thickness of gel coat is sprayed in to start with. Then once the laying-up procedure is complete, the operator applies a vacuum, which holds the paired mould tools together – and the panel production is under way.

The door lining, the door inner and the door outer panels are fabricated here; they are bonded together as one moulding. Luke indicated a nickel-based tool, which is the luxury end of the mouldings market – a very expensive item that provides a particularly high-class finish. It is a very durable mould, capable of being cleaned very quickly with abrasive products, unlike the plastic-based moulds that require considerable care when cleaning off of waxes and styrene produced during curing.

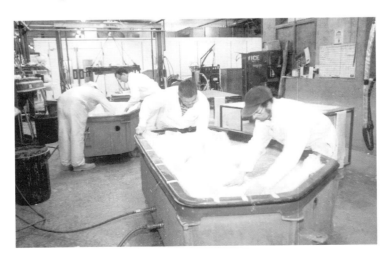

Operators load the glass-fibre mat patterns into the body side moulding tool after the gel coat has been applied.

Nickel-faced tools are manufactured in the Lotus tool room, and this shows an Elise inner door mould being readied for resin injection.

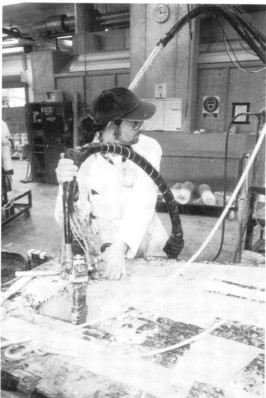

Two main types of resin are used in the injection process. As well as a general-purpose version, there is a low-profile resin, which is being used here; this has a faster cycle time and produces a higher-quality panel.

Water-based detergent cleaners are used these days rather than solvents.

Lotus are trying to reduce the amount of waste that occurs with each moulding. Fibreglass panels have traditionally built up a relatively high proportion of waste or flashing in the creative process, which needs trimming off. So Lotus are moving towards 'high investment' groups of tooling, something that a mainstream manufacturer like Renault may use, with which they can squeeze out complete panels as a finished wing or bonnet. Luke Bennett explained:

> At the moment Lotus do not have the luxury of highly expensive presses, but we have more basic clamps, which, when applied to the mould tool whenever there is an aperture to be cut away, seal the resin going into the mould, thereby cutting down on waste resin. So that's the kind of thing we are now moving into. We call it a 'near net moulding'. There will still be some trimming to do, but it'll be minimal.

In order to avoid the need for presses, Lotus had to design a mould tool with a press built into it: underneath the moulds

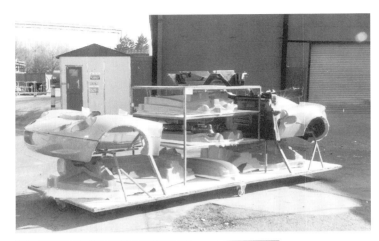

A complete kit of Elise body panels travels on a trolley from the body moulding shop to the body machining department.

Loading the moulded door inner panels onto robot machining centre bucks for trimming. The robot uses a water jet to cut wheelarches and apertures. Notice the vacuum cups that are used to hold the panel in position during moulding.

are devices like inflatable balloons, resembling air bags made of high-strength vulcanized rubber. Big straps pass through the mould tool, and when inflated the bags clamp the mould tool together. They provide a pressure of about four tons each, and there are sixteen to a press. The mould tool in question is called an RTM (resin transfer moulding), and it's used for manufacturing the crash structure for the front end of an Elise, so it has a very high glass-to-resin content – about 50 per cent glass and 50 per cent resin. A normal moulding would be about 35 per cent glass to 65 per cent resin. Because it's contains a lot glass – which is very strong – the mould takes a lot of clamping down.

BODY TREATMENT

The panel sets for the Elise bodies go from the body moulding shop into body machining, passing from one department to another across an access road aboard a trailer. Here, the panels are prepared for painting, and the first operation that greets them is the trimming facility. The Elise body parts are machined up in a booth on a water jet cutter, which trims off

The operators ensure that the door inner panels are correctly located onto the buck. The robot cutter is at the rear centre.

all the waste flashing to produce a cleanly finished panel. This is done by a typical robot with a water jet cutter on the end of its arm, fed with pressurized water to 5,000psi. It is a very noisy process.

There are several heavy-duty machine tools here, including punch presses, flanging presses and welding jigs to manufacture the steel rear subframe. As we have seen, the reason the subframe is made of steel is for the strength required to carry the engine and suspension pick-up points. It is also hot-dip zinc galvanized, both as a rust preventative and to solder the assembly together. It's evident that there is added strength where the soldering occurs, because of the special properties of zinc. Components are galvanized by a company in Essex, and deliveries take place once a week. Its sections are made on a DNC (direct numerically controlled) punch press

Alan Sterry assesses the quality of an Elise rear subframe prior to the commencement of another job on the CNC punch press.

An operator monitors the folding of a batch of Elise handbrake channels after the punch-press procedure has taken place.

The operator is setting the panels for the rear subframe in a jig where they are clamped prior to welding.

acquired in 1998, a machine designed to make small batches of fairly intricate parts, programmed by an operator who sits in the office and downloads the programme. Luke summed it up:

We are doing 900 hits (functions) a minute, 900 beats a minute. It is unlikely you can get it to do that in normal manufacture, because of the complexity of the shapes you do, but, if you're doing a series of holes, one after the other, it's possible to do 900 hits a minute. On average it probably does about 300.

Nearby was a ten-year old machine tool said to be capable of about a hundred functions, indicating how far the technology has come. The new one's tool head can be rotated, so a variety of angles can be cut simply by turning its head. Apart from the Elise rear subframe and the handbrake channel, the Esprit chassis are also produced here. Luke continued:

We bought this piece of machinery at the same time as the new tool. It's a DNC folding press and it can calculate angles of fold. In this case it's fairly simple because it's folding up a 90 degree bend, but in

With the sections for the rear subframe clamped in their jig, the operator then MIG-welds the assembly together.

Sparks fly as a fully masked and aspirated operator MIG-welds up an Elise wishbone in a jig.

many cases you are folding up less than 90 and it calculates the amount of force it needs to put on to be able to do that. It also calculates for naturally springy material how much it has to over bend to allow for spring back, so it's quite a sophisticated bit of kit.

We went on into the TIG welding area, and watched the operator in one bay manufacturing the Elise rear frame for which the machine tool had been slicing up the sections. The welders are masked up, obviously, and their helmets have a visor that is clear until the operator strikes an

arc; then the ultra-violet from the arc activates the liquid crystals in the visor and turns it blue to protect the operator's eyes from the dazzling light of the burning spelter.

In another couple of bays wishbones were being fabricated, and Luke was at pains to point out that they are what he called 'high accuracy' items, the result of very good jig work. He said that the operators are well trained to produce technically good welds. Not only do their joints look impressive but they are also porosity free – so moisture has no access to the inside of the tube. The wishbones are

After welding, wishbones are allowed to cool before leak detection and zinc plating.

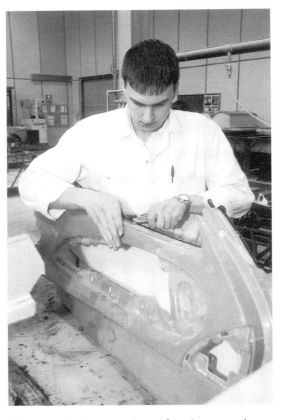

The operator is preparing a door inner section for bonding to a door outer panel.

zinc-plated by a local firm at Loddon, and in the process they are dipped in acid. But if the acid gets inside the tube they will rust out from the inside. After welding they are checked in a bath, to look out for bubbles. Any air expanding in the tube will create bubbles, in which case they will have to be reworked. Since there are eight wishbones to a car, this is a component that requires a high degree of accuracy.

Along with the wishbones, the rear subframes are made in quite sophisticated jigs. The operator fuses the Elise rear subframe by MIG welding, and the wishbone pick-up points are spot-welded on. Very high standards of accuracy are required because the wishbones locate there and the Elise suspension geometry is all-important. It complements the chassis, which is very accurate because it is a bonded structure and there is no distortion due to heat. The engineers can actually set the wheel geometry on the production line, whereas normally the vehicle has to be placed on its wheels to allow the bushes to settle.

The door components are bonded together in jigs to make a complete door. There are two preparatory jigs, where the catch plate and hinge mountings are bonded in using a rubbery polyurethane adhesive similar to the material used for

Here is a front crash structure curing in the bonding jig.

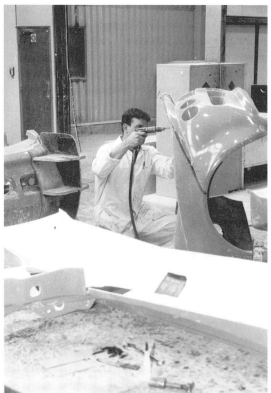

An operator finishes the fettling of an Elise rear clamshell, here drilling the hole for a harness clip.

bonding car windscreens. Similar jigs relate to the rear clam, front clam, bonnet, engine cover, and the front crash structure with the high glass ratio, which will eventually have the radiator mounted on it. The bucket seats are machined here too, and brackets and seat belt mountings are bonded in; they are trimmed in leather later.

An alarm goes off, reminding me that the noise level in here is already quite high – though nothing like as deafening as the Morgan tin-shop, which is my personal high-decibel yardstick. I don't hear the normally ubiquitous Radio One at this point, but listen hard and you can just about hear it in the background. As in all such plants, the operators like to have a radio on as it keeps the day ticking along. It's much more evident in the assembly area, and apparently there are regular debates as to whether the workers should listen to Radio One, Radio Norfolk, or Radio Broadland.

The next area we visit is the paint shop. A selection of panel sets stood waiting for the paint shop, which runs on double shift (the assembly shop runs a single shift). I

Operators load seat shells into a bonding jig after robot machining has taken place.

noted that a number of green cars were going through, following a handful of blue ones. Colour batching is inevitable because it avoids contamination going from one colour to another in quick succession, and that way the guns and equipment don't have to be cleaned constantly.

The body panels are all mounted on trolleys, and when they enter the paint shop, they first get two coats of primer. After that they go on decks and have any imperfections sanded off, after which they get another coat of primer. There is then another opportunity for any flaws to be dealt with before the panels proceed along the back wall of the paint shop to get their colour and clear coat. This is carried out in sealed booths by fully masked operators who wear respirators. They can be seen at work through thick glass panels, working quickly around the panel sets, moving the spray gun from side to side as they go. In total there are four passes of paint, comprising two coats each. Luke Bennett explained new trends in the painting process.

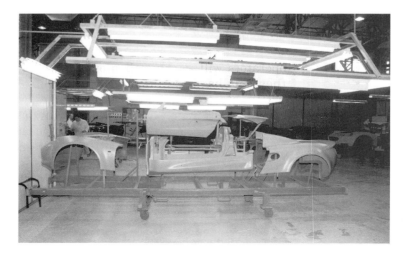

An Elise body-in-primer awaits inspection prior to receiving its colour and clear coat. This is part of a spot-check procedure, with perhaps one unit a day being selected.

A general view of the paint shop, with primed body panels resting on their jigs before going off for colour and clear coat.

Primed clamshells, doors and body panels are rubbed down with sanding discs to ensure there is a good key for the colour coat.

Because of EC regulations, we are using a super high solid primer, 80 per cent solid by weight, a super high solid clear coat, again 80 per cent solid by weight, and a water-based base coat. So everything has gone water-based, because it's not just the primer or the colour or the clear coat that has to be compliant – it has to be a totally compliant system.

Once a panel set has received its colour and clear coat, it emerges from the paint oven on a little rail, having been baked at 80°C for eighty minutes. There are now three options: a 'gun-finished car' can go straight on to the assembly line. Alternatively, it may have some minor 'nibs' that the operators will swiftly polish out; at worst, they may have to do a respray, which is a pretty catastrophic state of affairs and very rare. Occasionally the third situation arises where the operators have to do a 'blow-in' on a small area. This may result from atmospheric contamination, although this is also rare because all the work is carried out in a clean-room environment where everybody wears white paper overalls, and every door has a double entry system to exclude any dust.

Operators at work in the painting booths, applying UHS (ultra-high solid) clear coat as part of the VOC (volatile organic compounds)-compliant paint system. Each car receives four coats of primer, two colour coats and two clear coats of lacquer to achieve what is known as a 'gun finish'.

The operators check the finished painted body for quality. Every car is inspected, and all blemishes are highlighted and appropriate remedial action taken.

'Cleanliness is the key to this whole operation,' said Luke. As we did our factory tour, Lotus was still at an early stage in its transition to water-based paints.

Every Friday since Christmas [1997] we have been doing water-based paint trials. We call Friday water-base day. By slowing the process down one day a week, we can actually put the cars through at a very slow pace and we must have about twenty cars out in the field with water-based paint on them. What we've got to do is to get the guys ready, get the feel of the equipment, get the operators trained – and actually two of these cars that stand here are ready for those trials.

These vehicles are prepared in a different fashion. The operators use a finer grade sand paper, and if the car is going to be painted in a light colour in water base, they apply a white primer because the opacity of water base white is low, meaning you have to provide a white background. Similarly, if it is a dark water base colour we are probably going to have to put on a dark primer. So we will end up with three primer shades, a grey, a white and a black. The film build on water-based paint is very small, typically about 30 microns, whereas on a traditional paint finish it is probably about 60 to 80 microns. It is just like painting with emulsion in effect. It is literally very watery. So the name of the game is to get maximum colour with a minimum application of paint.

BURLY CHASSIS

We were now moving into the main assembly area, where attention first focuses on the chassis. Until chassis production switched from Denmark to Herefordshire, the chassis arrived on pallets on a curtain-sided transporter. The chassis are not 'handed' one way or the other, so any one of them can be made into a right- or left-hand drive car. My guide recapped some of the main points about the Elise chassis construction:

When an extrusion is placed across the lines, it provides a bond gap. There's nothing that needs adjusting subsequently. The lines in the extrusions provide a slot for the body to plug into,

making an accurate jigging point. In certain places the extrusions are split so it can be adjusted, because there is a tolerance across the extrusion to maintain the bond gap.

The glue is used as a sealant as well as a bonding material. There is a lot of surplus glue to be seen at some bonding points, and this is not a problem because they will eventually be hidden away. On the inside of the chassis there is very little glue showing because it is an A-class area of the vehicle, that is, most of it is visible. Nearly every joint is consolidated with an Ejot fastener, which is like a sophisticated self-tapping screw. Ejot is another partner from the building industry that came on board with Hydro Aluminium.

The chassis are made of high quality 6000 aluminium, and all components are anodized, not out of necessity but because this is the pre-treatment for the bonding process, and it also gives a more durable finish against corrosion. As we have already seen, the rear chassis section is made of steel and is hot-dip anodized. This process has the effect of making it long-term corrosion proof and it also solders the

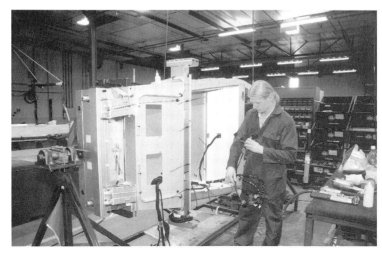

In the initial stages of assembly the chassis is dressed with wiring harnesses and coolant pipes. At this stage the only thing that determines the specification of the vehicle is the wiring harness.

joints and makes them even more durable. It may seem that a major steel component on a chassis made of aluminium is somewhat incongruous, but it was necessary because there would otherwise need to be spreader plates or washers to get the high load points out into the structure. At the rear of the car you'd end up with so many washers that it would be easier to weld the sections together. So it was made out of steel instead.

During the first two stages down the line the chassis are being dressed and fixtures (or jigs) enable the chassis to be turned over so that the gear linkages, handbrake cables and wiring harnesses can be fitted. I ventured to say that perhaps I might have expected the suspension to be the first elements to be fitted, but he replied that accessibility was the key. Harnesses do tend to be installed first at the body-in-white stage in most car plants, but as the Elise has a separate chassis unit, unusually these days, I thought perhaps this might be different. Indeed the Esprit is different, in that the systems on the Elise go on the chassis, whereas on the Esprit they are installed in the body: its steering column, seats and so on are fitted to the body and the chassis is plugged in underneath. The Elise bodywork, on the other hand, is just superficial clothing as far as the mechanicals are concerned. Luke motioned me over to the extrusions for the uprights, originally made by Hydro Aluminium. He said:

> The trick is to get the voids in it. You're obviously familiar with a tube of toothpaste. Well the material squeezed out of it doesn't have a hole in it. What you need in order to make a hole in your extrusion is a mand, and the mand has to be held to the outside of the die to create the hole. You end up with something like an aerofoil section, which goes on to the die itself for the aluminium to flow through and rejoin. If you imagine the outside of the die is a hole, but all the 'holes' have to have the 'aerofoils' attached to their perimeter. As the aluminium is pushed through the die, its progress is interrupted by the holding attachments. The pressure has to be high enough in order for the aluminium to weld itself back together again after it has passed through the attachment.

General view of the Elise assembly line. The car in the foreground is in the final stages of completion, and is about to have its seats installed.

At this stage the Rover K-series engine is dressed for fitting into the Elise. This includes equipping it with the appropriate exhaust down pipe, Elise cam-covers and Lotus dipstick.

Lotus found that on very heavy extrusions with thick walls that they needed a 13,000-ton press, and the only place where one was available was Aluswisse in Switzerland. Consequently these raw extrusions were manufactured in Switzerland, cut to length and shipped to the chassis manufacturer.

RIOTOUS ASSEMBLY

The long, spacious assembly area is an environment in which the senses are bombarded by the spectacle of myriad car components, all in a state of flux. There are engines, drivetrains and recognizable Elise panels, air tools and suspended air lines, parts bins, racks, jigs, ramps, and bustling operators putting things together, to the muffled accompaniment of the current hit records.

There are sixteen build stages in the production of the Elise, which is produced at a rate of one unit every thirty-six or seven minutes. The first stage deals with the aluminium chassis, which receives its wiring loom and suspension componentry. It is then married up with a Rover K-series 1.8 powertrain, which weighs about 220lb

The neat pedal box assembly demonstrates further use of extrusion technology: the clutch, brake and accelerator pedals all come from the same extrusion, and are machined to different widths for their specific applications.

Adhesive is applied to the dash baffle for fitment prior to the bonding of the body sides.

The operator fits the rear uprights and hub assembly, complete with wishbones. All aluminium-to-steel interfaces are protected to avoid electrochemical corrosion.

(100kg). It is exactly the same as the MGF power unit, except that Lotus makes slight modifications for its own installation, and the dipstick tube carries the Lotus logo on the top of it.

CONTINUOUS RECYCLING

Some components, such as fixings, are delivered by the supplier to the point of use and sit in blue bins until needed, and they never have to come through the stores. For example, a supplier called Newfast Industrial Fasteners brings fixings from its warehouse in Peterborough twice a week to the point of use on the Elise assembly line, in a continuous recycling process. Luke explained that the line was about as condensed as they could have it for the volume of cars they were producing: 'Obviously the more line stages you have, the more value you have tied up in work in progress, and the name of the game is to minimize that.'

We examined the extrusions for the pedals. 'It is really pleasing to eye isn't it? Whatever action the pedal performs is what goes on the brake. No servo assistance, no power steering, none of that jazz,' said Luke. The brake pedal is identical to the clutch pedal, which is the same as the throttle pedal, which is a bit thinner – the same extrusion but two-thirds the width. It is also exceedingly light. The die for the pedal boxes and pedal extrusions costs about £1,500, which is relatively inexpensive, in that it produces three pedals. Tony Shute is justifiably pleased about the value for money these extrusions provide. 'The McLaren F1 pedal die costs about £1,000, so we are getting excellent value for money.'

Other components we had seen being manufactured, like the handbrake channel and the wishbones, were being fitted, and it was gratifying to see these finally being located on the vehicle. Here was a chassis with its rear frame ready to receive the engine and wishbones. Luke indicated the only press on the line, which consists of a green frame with a piston coming out of it, manned by a single operator who is active all day. The press's frame, designed in-house, fabricates the suspension uprights. Luke explained how it worked:

The operator manufactures one set of

parts on the press, presses together the bushes, the ball joint, presses the bearings into the hubs, delivers them by trolley to the next car, and takes away an empty trolley. It's known as a one-piece flow. We are trying not to have quantities of these all assembled ready to be fitted, because all the value is just tied up. One-piece flow means you receive from your supplier, you make one piece, fit it and move it to your customer. It's not like the Japanese kanban system where you order material from the stores and from fabrication when you've still got components to hand.

The Elise brake discs are made of metal matrix composite – aluminium and silicon, which is incredibly light compared with the cast iron of traditional brake discs. The brakes endow the car with pin-sharp stopping capability, and yet run at very low temperatures because aluminium is an excellent heat conductor (as opposed to steel, which is an excellent heat absorber). The operating principle of the brakes is that the material of the pad migrates to the surface of the disc, and builds a deposit on the disc, so that it actually gets thicker

The body side mouldings are bonded to the chassis along with the windscreen and its surround using polyurethane adhesive. Including initial cure of the adhesive, this operation takes place in a 36-minute cycle.

Operators ensure that all critical safety features are secure using torque wrenches.

Suspension fasteners are tightened and torque-checked after the car's suspension geometry has been verified as accurate. At the bottom left is the alignment equipment.

during the course of its life and then gradually reduces again. Though this is not a requirement for the Elise, it may be possible to design a pad and disc that last the lifetime of the car.

So far all the stages we have seen are to do with dressing the chassis, which is similar to what happens in traditional car plants. Now we reach the point at which the body sides go onto the chassis, which is probably unique in the entire motor industry. They locate into slots in the chassis sides and towards the inside of the car. With the chassis locked in its jig, the A- and B-pillars fit into the sills and are

plugged in with complete accuracy, and are located to the screen frame and the roll hoop. The front crash structure, a special item in itself, also goes on at this point. The cables and piping around this jig control the system, while hot air is blown at 70°C onto critical points along the bond joints to increase the rate of cure on the polyurethane adhesive. In effect it spot welds the panels and chassis together to allow them to progress faster than if they were simply air-dried, and a few judiciously placed auxiliary heaters speed things up even more. The emergent body-chassis unit is hard enough to dejig after thirty

Suspension fasteners are tightened and torque-checked after the car's suspension geometry has been verified as accurate. At the bottom left is the alignment equipment.

The car is now really starting to take shape as two operators fit the rear clamshell.

This operator is installing the Stack instrument panel in a left-hand drive car.

The doors are completely sub-assembled before they are fitted to the car by Ian Sabberton and his team. Use of extrusions is again evident in the door hinge assembly.

Doors are accurately aligned to the body using assembly jigs to ensure a precise fit.

Wherever possible, parts are sub-assembled prior to final fitment to the vehicle. Here, the rear lights and fuel filler neck are fitted to the rear clamshell, and, below, the headlights go into place in the front clamshell.

Almost at the end of the assembly line, this Elise reveals its rear suspension system, engine and gearbox assembly and exhaust layout. This is the only stage in the assembly process where the car is on the ramp. The wheels and wheelarch liners are fitted at this stage, but the diffuser panels that form the rear undertray have yet to be installed.

and clamp the panels in place, where they remain until the adhesive goes off. The windscreen glass, which comes from Rio Glass in Spain, is installed after the jig is shut. Throughout this operation, the operators perform like a well co-ordinated football team. You can watch them for ages to see how it's accomplished, yet still be mystified by their impressive dexterity.

The next piece of apparatus we see is the wheel angle equipment, on which the operators check wheel angles, camber, castor, toe-in. Naturally it is very accurate, and they set it up and simulate the ride height with a fixed strut in place of the spring and damper. This is the first model that Lotus has been able to set up on line, and they can be sure that it will still be good once it is on its wheels.

'The back uprights have add-on bits,' Luke said. 'The nice thing is you can change the camber without upsetting the toe-steer. The two are quite independent.' It is also what Luke described as 'a low-activity stage', in so far as the operator is working on the wheel corners rather than clambering over the car. This means that the adhesive is given a bit more time to go off, though it still takes about a day for the glue to go off totally.

When the jig fixtures come off, the Elise centre section is virtually complete, and the car is now drivable. An advantage to Lotus is that the styling of the car can be updated very easily, simply by redesigning the front and rear clamshells – the boot and bonnet if you like – and retaining the standard chassis and central panels. This was one of the original design tenets, to allow for facelifted panels at a later date.

The windscreen wiper is bolted in place, and the heater ducts are installed at this stage. The door beams are inserted, followed by all the seals and window runners. The check-strap is also a neat

minutes. Another advantage of bonding is that the joint does not distort, and this is particularly advantageous for suspension pick-up points. On the Elise they are within half a millimetre, compared with the Esprit chassis on which they may be out by plus or minus 3mm.

Fitting these panels is a complex, fast-moving procedure, involving the jig's detachable side gates and the high-precision guide rails that slide into the jig

The soft-tops are fabricated at the bottom end of the assembly line, and the material sub-assemblies are sewn together here.

A seat is readied for final trimming, having its foam cushions applied.

The Elise seats are made in-house. Here, David George is multi-cutting foam for the padding.

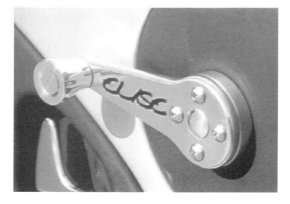

The Elise Sport window winder has neat detailing.

A freshly completed car, body panels covered in protective cladding, is put through its paces on the Hethel test track to check that all systems are functioning correctly.

section of gauze. We watched the doors being mounted, and again I suspect the operators make it look easier than it really is. They use equipment known as the door-setting jig; a ready-assembled door, complete with impact beams, is mounted off its guide pins and the jig allows the operator to approach the car holding the door while holding it up, to attach the hinges to the chassis. The one-piece body sections take about ten minutes to bolt on, and they are fully assembled with lights and indicators. The final stage on the assembly line is called 'vehicle run-up', which is the first time the key is turned and the engine fired up. Extractor pipes remove the exhaust fumes. After a test run, the bodywork will receive a final polish in the dispatch area.

All the seats are upholstered and trimmed here, and the soft-tops are manufactured in a semicircular area at the far end of the assembly shop. The fabrics are dispensed from rolls of material and are marked out and cut using templates on spacious workbenches. The canvas-type material is cut out using templates as guides on a bench at the rear, and it is sewn together in an area called a horseshoe. Part of the road test includes a visit to the water test rig, where the car is doused with water to test for leaks, a test the soft-tops invariably pass under normal driving conditions.

As we left the assembly line en route to the well-stocked factory restaurant we passed the test track. Several Elise and Esprit models were circulating at fairly modest pace. Lotus has two test drivers on site. Luke commented:

They give them two or three laps, and it gives us the opportunity to see that the car is running perfectly with no squeaks or rattles or anything like that. We also think the customer is prepared to pay for that as a part of the Lotus build process, to be able to say that the car has been evaluated on the track.

3 Chassis Engineering

So much of what Lotus do – and always have done – is about handling and excellence of car dynamics that this chapter is fundamentally germane to the Elise. Without the expertise of Lotus's chassis development people the Elise could not be the gem that it is. Historically Lotuses have always outshone their contemporaries in the ride and handling department. Leaving

When the author drove a 1994 Esprit Turbo S4 on the MoD's Chobham track in a back-to-back test, it felt more surefooted than the other 'supercars' ranged against it. But would the Elise feel even more poised?

aside that overworked debate about build quality, the Excel was a more driver-friendly – and therefore more engrossing – car to drive than the Porsche 944 that it was inevitably compared with. The Esprit felt more alive and more sure-footed than the Honda NSX, Porsche 911 and Toyota Supra that I drove at the Chobham test track during a back-to-back feature for *CarWeek* magazine in 1994. To find out how they made the Elise equally as competent – if not superior – to its predecessors, I talked to the movers and shakers in the Lotus Chassis Development Group.

Stephen Swift is the manager of the Chassis Development Group, which is all about vehicle dynamics. Like Roger Becker, John Miles and Morris Dowton he has been there a long time and is steeped in Lotus tradition. Roger and John have had a huge input into the character of Lotus cars for many years as far as handling dynamics is concerned, so they are very well respected. When the car was first conceived they were very much in on the concept of it and how the car was going to be used, and helped to push it through and convince the senior management that it was the car they should be building. Tony Shute was in control of the project from day to day and he has also done a lot of development driving. He too once worked in the Chassis Development Group and is a great Lotus enthusiast, so he knew instinctively that this was the sort of car that Lotus needed to build.

Back in 1988, the engineering staff operated from a Portakabin rather than the austere building they inhabit now, and

One of the prime movers in the 'step-in car' and the Elise project was Lotus's head of chassis engineering Roger Becker, about to take one out for a test drive. One of Roger's roles is that of facilitator – he gives licences to allow projects to get off the ground, like Chris Boardman's Olympic bike, for example.

where much of the material for this chapter was gleaned. Austere it may be, but you start to feel the history oozing out of it when Steve tells you that it was where Colin Chapman built his Moonraker cabin cruisers, and where in 1979 they built the first DeLoreans. It started off as an aircraft hangar in the Second World War, and it became home for Chassis Engineering in 1996. But even this is temporary accommodation, and they will move to somewhere more 'palatial' in the new site.

We started off talking about the original ideas for the Elise. As we have heard, it was originally meant to be a sort of step-in car, with no doors, along the lines of a Lotus Seven, or dare I say it, a beach buggy. Lotus recognized that if they could produce one, they would save an awful lot of weight, money, and engineering time in making doors. But when they looked at the practicalities, it just wasn't feasible. It is not the easiest of cars to get in and out of even now, so a higher sill would have been even more difficult to surmount. That still left the issue of weather protection unanswered.

Lotus looked at having one wind-down window, for example, but factors such as car park and toll booths made that idea impractical. However, an awful lot of engineering goes into one window and the roof of the car and it can take a lot longer than sorting out ride and handling. The detailed work of putting in a window to go up and down and using as many parts off the shelf as possible is actually very difficult. They were trying to make something that was cheap to build, and doors and windows that go up and down create a lot of complexities. Steve Swift illustrated the point about Lotus engineers being all-rounders. 'We have to get involved with absolutely everything,' he said, 'but that does make it very exciting because we are involved with the car as a whole, and that gives you a sense of ownership and a sense of pride in the car.'

Again I'm getting the message about Lotus people being all-rounders, and in this instance it meant that the engineering guys liaised with other departments, including design, where the potential for conflict loomed over certain details. For instance, the car's point of contact with the road is its tyres, and they needed to give serious consideration to the wheels. After all, people spend a small fortune customizing their cars with aftermarket wheels, so it was something Lotus could get right from the start. The wheels needed to be distinctive and unique to Lotus, so it was worth investing money in them to get them right. They are made by AWI in Wales, although they were designed in house.

TYRE INSIDER

Besides the tyre they fit as standard, car manufacturers approve perhaps two other makes for the vehicle; if the customer then goes out and fits something that's a bit cheaper, it may well ruin the car's handling. You shouldn't always assume that tyre fitters are competent either. It may seem an obvious point, but when directional rotation tyres – Goodyear Eagle F1 – were fitted on the wrong sides of my Alfa 155, it behaved like a gazelle in panic under heavy braking, but its manners were restored once the mistake was corrected. You can get lucky though. A few years ago I was fortunate to discover that Yokohamas transformed the

handling of my old rear-wheel drive Alfa 75 into something far more elegant and dance-worthy than the Michelins it was originally supplied with. Mind you, tyre evolution could well have reversed that particular position by now. So while ordinary family cars are obviously very sensitive to tyres, a sports car is doubly susceptible to variations in surface and dynamics. The lower the profile of the tyre, the more sensitive it becomes. Wide tyres with shorter sidewalls make the car much more sensitive to all the suspension parameters, and the steer effects, kinematic steer, and shock absorber damping all become much more significant.

Clearly the car is set up with brand new tyres, but 10,000 miles (16,000km) worth of wear would affect an Elise more than it would a regular car. The wear ratio of the Elise is likely to be about two sets of rear tyres to one at the front. 'We recognized the fact that we had to put decent-sized boots on the thing just from the aesthetics point of view,' said Steve. 'Tyre technology is currently focused on cars that weigh a third more than the Elise, so together with Pirelli we were pushing the technology envelope quite a bit.'

It may look racy, but because its chassis is welded rather than bonded, the Renault Sport Spider weighs a relatively hefty 2,068lb (940kg). According to certain Lotus commentators, there was little point in making its chassis out of aluminium, since its performance on the race track from 160bhp is inferior to the 120bhp Elise, which weighs in at a far lighter 1,584lb (720kg).

Lotus cars have always been special in one way or another. The modern Elan was able to get lots of power down without suffering from all the disturbing influences that pertain with front-wheel drive, while the Esprit was an object lesson in how to get maximum power out of a relatively small engine. The Elise on the other hand has something for everybody, and the engineering guys are also keen to get the message across. 'The main reason why we've got all these features in the car, particularly the chassis and the brakes, is because it's an engineering shop window,' said Steve, 'which enables us to say that we are the first company in the world to productionize these items.'

Without further ado I was whisked off down to the workshop, where a great deal of strictly confidential work on clients' vehicles goes on. A lot of the diagnostic equipment that is used on a regular basis lives in here or nearby. There is instrumentation for interior noise assessment and modal performance, and equipment for vehicle alignment, which is apparently the best you can buy. There is also a shaker platform, and probably what is the most complex collection of equipment of all – the compliance rig. Steve explained:

> As far as chassis development is concerned, this is the most important piece of equipment here, and we built it ourselves. It enables us to distinguish all of the important suspension characteristics on a car. Basically we bolt the chassis to a rigid framework and then sit the wheels on platforms, which are like little hovercraft, so that the wheel can float and move to wherever it wants to. We then attach very accurate sensors to the wheel and apply loads to the platform similar to those seen when driving. The sensors can measure wheel rotations to within a hundredth of a degree, and displacements to about a tenth of a

millimetre, which allows us to see how the wheel and suspension behave when they encounter a bump, or when they are subjected to cornering loads.

With the ability to 'take the suspension apart' and measure all the important characteristics, which even Lotus didn't have the means to do a decade ago, it is possible to zoom in quickly on suspension problems during development and, more importantly, confirm that the intended suspension design has been realized in the car. Steve continued:

> For example, you might think you know what the spring rate is. But there are other 'springs' in the suspension – apart from the coil spring, the simplest example being the rubber bushes found in the suspension links; even the tyre itself is a spring. These are known as parasitic stiffneses and mean that the spring rate of the suspension might be different to what you anticipated. This machine allows you to find out exactly what's there, so you can confirm that what you've designed is what you've built. We've had plenty of clients' cars in here where that hasn't been the case, where what they built is different to what they designed, even to the extent of the wheels steering in the wrong direction from suspension movement, which is pretty fundamental.

I venture to comment that it's not quite as bad as if you turn left and the car goes right. Steve replied:

> Not quite, but not far off. There are a lot of very subtle things that affect the way a car behaves. For example, compliance steer, which is to say, how the wheels steer in response to a cornering force, can have a huge affect on steering response and limit handling behaviour even though the steer

Probably the most complex collection of equipment is the compliance rig, which enables Lotus's chassis engineers to define all the important chassis characteristics. (Courtesy of Lotus Cars)

While the compliance rig is used for obtaining optimum suspension settings, these are fine-tuned on the production line.

angles concerned are incredibly small.

Historically it was quite a difficult thing to measure, but with this equipment you can do it very easily, so the Elise spent a fair amount of time on here while we were getting to understand it.

Over the years the compliance rig has confirmed to us that one of the secrets of successful vehicle dynamics lies in the ability to set up the suspension consistently. This was one of the design objectives of the Elise, and the geometry is so well controlled that they can test two different Elises on the rig and get almost identical results for the important suspension characteristics.

Quite clearly, the development engineer is now in a position that would have been unthinkable ten years ago, and has taken a lot of the hit and miss out of vehicle development. And the time span between the inception of a concept and a well-proven car is dramatically reduced, which is a significant bonus for Lotus's consultancy work.

CHASSIS GURU

I couldn't but help feeling that I was in the company of a minor deity when John Miles came in. I mean, you'd be at home down the local over a pint of beer with any of the engineering guys I met at Lotus, but Miles is somehow different. Although paradoxically his demeanour is at times verging on the diffident, an insouciant manner hides a real seriousness and depth of commitment to his work.

As a race fan in the 1960s, I used to see him regularly racing the Willment Elan and the works' Lotus 47. He drove the Lotus 41 F3 car in 1967 and 1968, and was entrusted with the development of the Lotus 63 four-wheel drive GP car. And of course he was Rindt's team-mate in the Lotus 49C and the new Lotus 72 F1 car, until his apprehensions about the 72's fragility were confirmed at Monza in 1970. Rindt was killed and Miles retired. So for me he's up there with the gods, and in any case there is a certain aura about him. He's been a Lotus chassis guru ever since his competition days, and now acts as a consultant based in a group called Control Systems, which is where active suspension came from, and where handling predictions

John Miles has been associated with Lotus and its racing cars since the mid-1960s, and he is retained as a chassis development consultant. He was one of the leading lights in developing the Elise from its origins in the 'step-in car' concept, and is seen here delivering a lecture for the author's benefit on the advantages of monotube shock absorbers over twin-tube dampers.

and suspension analysis take place.

'These subtleties have become increasingly important in making a car work well,' said John, 'and the important things that define a good or a bad car really are tyres, damping and steer effects.' These last can come in two forms: kinematic and compliant. These happen because when the suspension is attached to the car with rubber – even on the Elise, which has very

79

stiff rubber – there are steer effects due to the elasticity in the system.

These steer effects are very important to understand, because ultimately what makes a tyre hold the road is vertical load and slip angle. This is what happens when you turn the steering wheel or what happens as the car starts to turn. A tyre generates a slip angle in response to a vertical load and a lateral force. As soon as you go down the road, the vertical load on the tyres changes. Obviously when the front wheel hits a bump the vertical load increases, causing the suspension to increase its camber. The tyre then develops a thrust and tries to push the car in one direction or the other, and that's even before you turn the wheel to negotiate a corner. So that thrust has to be countered in some way otherwise the car won't behave itself.

John explained that, in broad terms, by introducing a steer effect when the bump occurs, you can reduce the deviation caused by the bump. In cornering, as soon as you turn the steering wheel, the load is transferred from one side to the other, so for example the load on the inside tyre is reduced and transferred to the outside tyre, thus increasing the vertical load on the outside tyre. At the same time the tyre is developing a slip angle and producing a lateral force; and the more vertical load you have, the more slip angle you have, and the more lateral force you have. Eventually you reach a point where the tyre becomes overloaded and you can get no more lateral force.

The wider the tyres you put on a car, the more interlocking points there are between the tyre and the road surface. The tyre generates grip by the rubber interlocking with the surface imperfections, and the rougher the road surface, the better the grip, so the wider the tyre, the more potential grip is available.

A lot of this may sound facile, but John was demonstrating how important it is to understand how to be able to control the loads on the tyres. Although you can't change the total weight transfer of a car once you have designed it, you can redistribute the tyre loads front to rear. Suppose, for example, that the car is oversteering. The engineers need to take some load out of the tyres because they are becoming overloaded and reaching their limit too soon. The normal remedy is to fit a front anti-roll bar or stiffer front springs, which will reduce oversteer by increasing the vertical load on the front tyres in a corner, that is, by shifting some of the cornering loads from the rear axle to the front axle; likewise with an understeering car you would want to shift tyre loads towards the rear to make the rear tyres do more work. It's a matter of redistributing the tyre loads.

There are other extraneous factors that affect understeer and oversteer, such as luggage or people in the back that make the car feel unstable, but that can be driven partially by the steer effects going on. It is usually easier to sort out a sports car because you don't have the massive load changes that you have in a hatchback, while in the case of the Elise, the mid-mounted engine position raises problems of rearward weight distribution and longitudinal displacement of the powertrain. John's metaphor to illustrate this was the one about whether you throw a hammer by the handle or the head. Head-first equals front-wheel drive, but rear-wheel drive is like trying to throw the handle first.

It was more difficult to make the Elise drivable over a wide speed range than it was with the Esprit, because of its more rearward weight bias: the Esprit is actually 55/45. The Elise has a 60/40 weight distribution, but it could be 50/50 if the engine was mounted longways. But of course it isn't, because that is how Rover supply the engine and gearbox. There has to be a compromise over the cost, because

Rover can either put the front-wheel drivetrain in the back or the front; the cost implications of installing the engine longways and making up the transmission for it would be monumental. They have to balance the input cost against the likely market price of the car, and in the final analysis, they have to settle for a standard front-wheel drivetrain. The Rover K-series unit thus becomes crucial to the design of the car because it's such a light engine.

CHAPMAN'S LEGACY

Traditionally, open cars have been structurally compromised, requiring a huge amount of stiffening to make them sufficiently rigid, but the Elise isn't at all like that, thanks to its aluminium extrusions chassis. John Miles made an apt appraisal.

It feels like a little racing car, and there was a strong element of going back to Chapman's early cars, where the core value was starting with a racing car, which was then made into a road car. The Six, the Seven, the Elite and the Eleven were all really racing cars but were just about usable on the road, and there was a strong feeling that we should go that way with the Elise. Whereas the Eclat and the Excel, all that range of luxury cars, and the modern Elan, were not the sort of car you would jump in and go to a hill climb with. That goes for things like the Boxster and the MGF, which are not what I would call sports cars, in the idiom of the 1930s when you got in a Riley Imp and took it to Brooklands and went racing with it. You can't really do that with an MGF or that kind of car as they weigh so much. The key to it is getting the weight down to something more like you would have in a racing car.

The Elise's light weight means that we

don't have to have servoed brakes, or power steering. The suspension componentry can be smaller, lighter and simpler. On the other hand, the Renault Spider weighs 940kg [2,068lb], and it has iron brakes and the accoutrements that a car of 940kg needs. According to Autocar tests, its circuit performance from 160bhp is slightly worse than the Elise's, which does the same thing on 120bhp, and this again is down to core Chapman philosophy.

By way of comparison, I note that the full rally-spec Renault Mégane weighs in at a comparable 960kg (2,112lb) as well.

John Miles made it sound as though once they'd settled on the design formula it was all straightforward, and there does seem to be an element of the inevitable about it: these guys just carry on inexorably until they've achieved perfection, or pretty well near to perfection.

As far as the suspension was concerned, some of the tuning knowledge came from the Esprit and the Elan, and obviously every time we work on a car we learn something, so we were able to predict the sort of characteristics that we needed. I don't think we changed anything kinematically, although we had to change the steer link at the back to make it stiffer. We tried alternative roll centres, but really none of them worked. We increased the initial castor angle because the steering was too light to give enough steering feedback. But after that we more or less left it alone. Originally the car was designed not to have a front anti-roll bar. But because we had to use a production tyre that was designed for a car with double the weight, we had to fit the front anti-roll bar to put more load into the front tyres to reduce the response and create some understeer.

Elise front suspension detail, showing chassis pick-up points, upper and lower wishbones, steering arm, Koni monotube damper, metal matrix ventilated disc, brake pipe, anti-roll bar, coolant pipe and part of front crash structure. The extruded aluminium suspension uprights are made by Aluswisse, as they are just too fat for Hydro to process.

YAW FREQUENCY

Early in the development programme it was felt that the Elise's response was too quick at high speed, so Lotus needed to build in some yaw damping to calm that down. At this point John went off on what appeared to be almost a medical tangent, which was nonetheless a fascinating excursion into hitherto (for me, at least) unknown aspects of vehicular physics.

He explained that everything has a natural frequency. If you push down on a stationary car and measure the response, it will have a natural frequency on its springs. The natural yaw frequency of a typical car is about 1.5hz,

which means that if you flick the steering and let go, it will oscillate one and a half times a second until it stops. The natural frequency of the Elise is 2.5hz because it is mid-engined, lighter, and because its tyres are stiffer (the tyres are effectively stiffer because it's light).

You just have to imagine that everything is a spring and a damper of some sort. Even the human body has natural frequencies: if I shake you and you are bouncing at 3–4hz you may feel sick because your internal organs are resonating. If you do this at about one hertz I believe you will feel seasick, because there are certain organs in your body which don't like that.

Now let's relate that to a car on the road situation. Let's take the A14 Newmarket by-pass (a fast three-lane highway) as a good example. There are some very bad truck grooves on the inside lane, and let's say you're driving along and the car gets upset by a groove. It suddenly dives a bit to the left or the right because of the groove. As the car deviates, you respond and try and correct that deviation, and the time you take from when you perceive the deviation to when you apply a corrective steering input is about one and a half seconds for the normal driver. It sounds like a long time, but it isn't. A racing driver can obviously reduce that response time, and he might operate at up to 3–4.5hz, but the normal driver is operating at about a 0.5–1hz. A car's natural frequency – even a normal car's – is higher than that, and the Elise is more than twice the frequency of a normal driver's operating regime, so it's very important to build some damping into the yaw behaviour. Some cars will want to diverge further and faster, while other cars will say 'no, just leave me alone and I will sort the problem out'. You don't have to be an expert to recognize that, because you know that certain cars feel safe in cross winds and in tramlines, while other cars feel nervous and unforgiving. Those differences in feeling are to do with the subtle steer effects that affect tyre slip angles at any given instant.

Lotus tried just four different types of stock tyre when developing the Elise; historically they have always carried out tyre tests because they are such an integral part of the suspension. As I implied earlier, the development of tyres in the last ten years has been enormous, and tyres have increased the sensitivity of steer effects, which are very influential on how a car

The Elise's attractive five-spoke alloy wheels were styled by the in-house design team, and made by Alloy Wheels International in Wales. They are shod with Pirelli P Zero tyres, unique to Lotus, measuring 185/55 R15 at the front and 205/50 R16 at the rear.

behaves. If you think of six different hatchbacks, you know that while there are differences in their suspension systems they all have struts at the front and maybe a twist beam or trailing arms at the rear. Two main things differentiate the good ones that drive nicely from the bad ones that get rubbished in the press. One is handling, and the other is ride quality. Peugeot scores highly on ride because they have control of the damping characteristics. They make their own dampers and they really understand what they are doing, whereas the big manufacturers, like GM and Ford, use outside damper manufacturers, so they are not so much in control of what goes on. Moreover, they don't have a chassis development group with the continuity of companies like Peugeot and Lotus. John commented:

> That's the way it is in order to progress in big manufacturers. They have to progress up the management structure in order to pursue a career, so they don't stay and tune cars. That's a lifetime's work for Lotus people. Chassis development is not something you can do suddenly. It would take you five to ten years to really begin to understand how the whole system works. It's that complex.

Indeed, it's a very intricate subject, but I think John explained it in layman's terms very well.

DAMPER TUNER

Now it appears we are getting down to the nitty-gritty, where the fine-tuning is carried out. The engineers at Lotus probably understand damper tuning at least as well as the tuners that work for the damper manufacturers, and at Hethel they have a special damper room, where John Miles delivered an impromptu lecture on the differences between monotube and twin-tube dampers. Twin-tubes are so-called because they've got two tubes inside them, while monotube dampers are of single tube design, basically lighter, and used in racing cars, where they can be mounted anywhere in the suspension set-up. The monotube was invented in the late 1950s and has several advantages over the twin-tube damper. Because the piston runs in the outer tube, it allows a very good damping capacity. The oil is in a sealed chamber, but

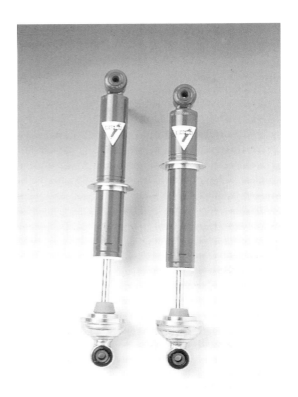

A pair of Koni monotube dampers as fitted on the Elise. The firm began making shock absorbers in 1932, and offers dampers for every make of car. Other makes, including Lamborghini, Dodge Viper and 1998 Tyrrell F1 cars, were also Koni-equipped.

if it were just a sealed chamber of oil, the damper wouldn't work, because if you tried to push the piston in and out it would just be solid. The monotube has a floating piston beneath the gas, which pushes the floating piston against the oil. When you pressurize the piston it compresses the oil, and if there is any gas there it just pushes it into the oil and makes it one solution. The end result is basically a gas-free column of oil. The gas has to be there under the floating piston to accommodate the change in volume.

The monotube is very consistent, and fade-free because there's no air inside. Apart from the fact that it's more expensive, the disadvantage of the monotube is that it has only got one valve (although that isn't wholly true because racing monovalves have another valve in a separate chamber, which is a more complex issue). Basically a monotube has only got one valve on the piston, and one leak path – that is, a low-speed leakage that allows the car to have just that bit of motion so it's not completely locked solid. That leak path is common to both compression and the rebound, which sometimes limits what you can do from the tuning point of view. 'If you change the leak path you affect the rebound and the compression, which is not the case in the twin-tube damper,' said John.

From a tuneability point of view the monotube is not as good as a twin-tube. Another disadvantage of the monotube is that the oil column is basically supported on a gas. In order for the damper to develop a force, it has to move the column of gas, so there is a compliant element in the damper that tends to inhibit the amount of roll-damping response you can achieve. John continued:

Now, in certain racing and rally cars this is not important, as all the roll-damping control is largely governed by the roll bars and very stiff suspension, whereas in the Elise we depend to an extent on damping for body control because we don't have a roll bar on the back. There is a limit to the front anti-roll bar stiffness, and in the Elise, we ended up with a situation where we were struggling a bit for roll control. The car's rate of roll is a bit quicker than is ideal, and that is the one disadvantage of monotube damping. We could improve it, but it would be at the expense of something else.

John revealed that in typical engineering projects that Lotus have carried out on a consultancy basis, they've made some eighty changes on the rear axle and perhaps a hundred on the front, and that's apparently quite normal as a step forward from what the manufacturer originally produced. They might even make more like 300 changes, because, as he says, the number of things you can change is endless.

Only by a process of change are you able to build up your knowledge. Everything you do is contributing to a data bank, and you can alter a tiny orifice, a leak path, by 1mm and it will totally change the car. For Lotus, damping is the most critical part of vehicle behaviour. Damping is probably more than 50 per cent of what a car feels like, and it is also probably the last of the black arts. When all else fails, it is the damping that has to sort the car out.

The other thing is that the monoubes tend to build more consistently than the twin-tubes. There are fewer parts and they are better made, and when you put them on the car from new there is much more chance of it being right. We've had endless problems in the past, but I think the Elise has almost been trouble-free from a damping point of view in production, with no leaks or anything like that, whereas the Elan was always in trouble with rejected dampers.

John Miles was involved with the concept of a new lightweight sports car from the outset.

Ken Sears, George Howard Chappell, Richard Hurdwell and I had this germ of an idea that became the step-in car. We were thinking initially about a composite car because we had some expertise in composites. I really didn't get involved in it much until the development stage, and

---

Putting a Damper on It

This potted history of the damper manufacturers Koni sheds a bit more light on an area that's pretty much overlooked by the majority of motorists. The Koni story goes back to 1857, when a Mr. A. de Koning started a saddlery in Oud-Beijerland in the Netherlands. In the early days they manufactured and repaired equestrian harnesses and upholstered carriages. After 1918, when the car became popular, small-scale production of radiator and spring covers was set up, with bodywork and paintwork on the side. From 1930 to 1940 Koni (as the company was by then known) mainly focused on the sale and maintenance of motorcars, as well as dealing in Chrysler, Renault, and Austin.

In 1932, production of friction dampers began, although this first production did not survive long, since American dampers were marketed in the Netherlands at knockdown prices during the Depression. The advent of the Second World War forced Koni to diversify into gas generators and a distribution valve to switch from petrol to gas. After the war they made garage equipment and car components like hydraulic jacks and adjustable shock absorbers. Koni have since developed into a company with branches in various countries, employing over 1,000 people, and exporting to more than ninety countries.

Koni make dampers for every make of car, and drivers can choose from the red Koni Special or the yellow Koni Sport dampers. For vintage cars there is the black Koni Classic damper. And although Koni have traditionally been linked with the replacement market, a growing part of their damper production is destined for standard fitment. Apart from Lotus, marques including Lamborghini and the Dodge Viper and Prowler are also Koni-equipped. The firm's association with motorsport competition goes back a long way, and it sponsored the 1998 Tyrrell F1 cars of Tora Takagi and Ricardo Rosset, which served as mobile test beds.

The fastest trains in the world run with Koni dampers as well: the French TGV is capable of speeds of 320mph (515km/h), while at a more prosaic level, Koni also supply vast quantities of shock absorbers to the Chinese Ministry of Railways. Koni dampers are also fitted on trams and underground trains in Amsterdam, London, Paris, Hong Kong and Singapore. Koni also make a special range of high-quality motorcycle dampers for motorcycles. There are special Koni dampers for trucks, trailers, buses, vans and all-terrain vehicles. These units include high-precision damping characteristics that are fine-tuned for nearly every type and make. After long periods of use, the dampers can be readjusted.

Dampers have some quite exceptional uses, outside the automotive industry. The Erasmus Bridge in Rotterdam is a cable-stayed bridge, half a mile (800m) long, which is equipped with special heavy-duty Koni shock absorbers. Each one is one metre long, and 12cm in diameter. The dampers prevent the thirty-two stay-cables from vibrating in strong crosswinds. Koni dampers were also used in the construction of the 8-mile (5km) long Zeeland Bridge. In order to absorb contraction and expansion, sets of 275lb (125kg) dampers were fitted between the separate bridge elements.

---

fairly late on, when it was with Dave's assistance. Tony Shute then took up the idea and it became the Elise.

One of the first projects was crash tests, and we had to cover various legislation issues that had to be got out of the way before we could concentrate on any development. So some of our early prototypes were used to get the legislation issues addressed, otherwise we wouldn't have had a product; it's as simple as that. We concentrated on doing that, which is probably the reverse of what we've done historically, so that we could devote our time to getting the car set up right.

I think we were reasonably confident

that we could sort it, because the car is so simple and there wasn't anything insurmountable in what we had conceived. Some cars you really do have to redesign to get them through the legislation, but by and large we didn't have to do that, so we were pretty confident in leaving the tuning of the car until fairly late in the day.

The first time we drove the car, everybody was cock-a-hoop because it was already very amazing, straight out of the box. In the Elan's case, we were learning. I think we can honestly say that we were not only designing something that Lotus were unfamiliar with, but at the same time we were also trying to learn how to make a front-drive car. And we had to condense that learning curve into a couple of years as well as overcoming many problems with front-wheel drive.

I wanted to muddy the waters a bit, to reach back to the early 1970s, to a time when I was actively involved with Lotuses. I wondered whether there were any similarities or parallels to be drawn between the Europa

and the Elise, apart from the fact that the mid-engined concept is the same, and both are powered by relatively modest-capacity, off-the-shelf proprietary engines. It was also raced with much success as the Lotus 47 (by Miles and others, like Chris Meek), and like the Elise's GT1 derivative, the 2.0-litre Lotus 62 sports prototype of 1969 evolved from the Europa. My idea was immediately crushed, however. 'Well not really,' said John. So much for rose-tinted spectacles and the mists of time. I remembered the Europa as being great fun to muck about with.

There is so much about the Europa that's different really. Colin Chapman had very clear ideas about how the suspension should work, and those ideas wouldn't necessarily work today, particularly as regards kinematic and compliance steer. In the days of Chapman, all bump steer was straight up and down like a racing car, but nowadays we can't do that to a car because of the tyres. There isn't a car made today which has straight up and down bump steer and that is why we talk about

The Type 46/74 Europa was the first mid-engined Lotus road car. It was in production from 1966 to 1975 (9,230 units built) and was similar in concept to the Elise, being mid-engined and powered first by the stock 1,470cc Renault R16 engine and then, as pictured here in JPS livery, with the 1,558cc Lotus twin-cam engine. But factors like weight distribution, compliance steer, and major advances in tyre technology render any other comparisons futile.

kinematic and compliance steer because it is actually steer: it isn't no steer, it is steer. Also if you look at the rear suspension on the Europa, it had the driveshaft as the top link of the suspension, as did early Esprits. That simply wouldn't be acceptable nowadays if you want a stable car. Because the drive shaft is attached to the gearbox, and the engine has to be mounted very stiffly because it is taking cornering loads. It goes back to the old Chapman strut-type philosophy, where there was a trailing arm, a bottom link, and a driveshaft, the drive shaft also acting as the top link. They do that on the Jaguar XJS and XK8, but the suspension and the diff are all on a subframe so that they can be mounted very stiffly because the subframe is mounted to the car with rubber. In the case of the early Esprits, the problems were pretty horrendous because you either had lots of engine and road noise and the car handled reasonably well, or it was tolerably refined with pretty awful handling. So no, I think things have moved on immeasurably in the last twenty years.

A lot of this has come about because of the differences in tyres. When you consider that in 1964 I held the GT lap record round Brands Hatch at 59.8 seconds in a 1,650cc Diva GT, which weighed about 17cwt, had 130hp and racing tyres – and getting below a minute was really something. Nowadays you can take any old 1,800cc GTi on road tyres, which weighs nearly twice as much as the Diva, and go round Brands Hatch in around a minute, and that's really down to the development of tyres.

If any of the foregoing has seemed to pass a little way over your head, join the club. But to his credit, John explained that it had been a while before the light dawned for him too.

Nothing's perfect, but I think that the good things about the Elise far outweigh any faults, and in particular I don't think anybody will ever produce a car that's so light and complies with the crash tests and all the current legislation. The environment is becoming increasingly inhibiting for somebody doing something innovative, and the risks of being innovative are enormous. If the design went wrong in terms of crash testing, the only thing you could do is add weight to save it. The concept of the Elise didn't have to be changed because we have some very good people here on structures and crash testing, and a lot of thought went into how the car would perform in all theatres. The Elise was risky to do, but that's what Lotus thrive on.

Yet in a way, it wasn't such a risk if you consider the essential specification of modern motorcycles: lightweight frame and suspension technology, excellent handling, dynamite acceleration and instantaneous braking, coupled with manoeuvrability and parkability. That all adds up to a highly desirable machine, which is what the Elise is. It has a similar combination of qualities, which are principally down to its light weight, which only the specialists like Caterham or Westfield, and Tomita's conceptually similar Tommy Kaira ZZ can hope to match. The equally low volume Renault Sport Spider and Noble M10 require more horsepower to get the job done.

**Lotus Elise
1996 to date**

Layout
Two-seat mid-engined lightweight high-performance convertible sports car.

Engine
Cylinders	Four cylinders in line, mid-mounted transversely
Capacity	1,796cc
Construction	Aluminium engine block with aluminium cylinder head
Max. power	118bhp at 5,500rpm
Max. torque	165Nm at 3,000rpm
Bore and stroke	80mm x 89.3mm
Valves	Double overhead camshaft with hydraulic tappets
Fuelling	Fuel-injected, mapping unique to Lotus
Ignition	Motorola electronic ignition system, mapping unique to Lotus
Alternator	85A

Transmission
Manual 5-speed transaxle driving rear wheels, hydraulic clutch
First	3.167
Second	1.842
Third	1.308
Fourth	1.033
Fifth	0.765
Reverse	3.000
Final drive	3.938

Body
Composite body panels with detachable front and rear 'clamshells'; integral fixed headlamps.

Chassis
Lotus-designed spaceframe structure of epoxy-bonded sections of aluminium extrusions (built by Hydro Raufoss Aluminium) incorporating integral roll-over hoop.

Suspension
Double wishbones with single coil springs over monotube dampers all round. Lotus-patented uprights of extruded aluminium, made by Alusuisse.

Steering
Rack and pinion, non-power assisted.

Wheels
Type	Unique Lotus-designed 5-spoke, by Alloy Wheels International
Front	5.5 J x 15
Rear	7 J x 16

Tyres

Type	Pirelli P Zero, unique to Lotus
Front	185/55 R15
Rear	205/50 R16
Spare	T 115/70 R15 (option)

Brakes

282 mm diameter aluminium/metal matrix ventilated discs made by Lanxide Brembo, mounted outboard. Non-servo split hydraulic system supplied by Automotive Products, including unique Lotus/AP Racing opposed-piston front callipers.

Instrumentation

Analogue electronic unit comprising speedometer and tachometer with multi-function LCD readout incorporating fuel and coolant gauges, supplied by Stack Instruments.

Lighting

6in main beam headlamps. Optional auxiliary driving lamps.

Dimensions (in/mm)

Wheelbase	90.6/2,300
Front track	56.7/1,440
Rear track	57.2/1,453
Overall length	146.7/3,726
Overall width	67.0/1,701 (excluding mirrors)
Overall height	47.3/1,202
Ground clearance	6.3/160
Fuel tank capacity	8.8 gallons (40l)
Fuel grade	95 RON minimum
Unladen weight	1,485lb (675 kg)
Weight distribution	39/61 (% front/rear)

Performance

Maximum speed	124mph (201km/h)
0–62mph (100km/h)	5.9s
0–100mph (160km/h)	18.0s

Fuel Consumption (mpg/l/100km)

Urban	28.9/9.6
Extra-urban	49.9/5.7
Combined	39.4/7.1

Standard Equipment

Alloy road wheels (lockable), 3-way catalytic converter, coded signal immobilizer, cloth hood, unique Lotus/Nardi steering wheel, leather storage pockets, passenger footrest, boot storage bag.

Warranty

Twelve month unlimited mileage from factory. Aluminium chassis eight years warranty against perforation corrosion.

Servicing
First service 1,000 miles, thereafter 9,000 miles or annually.

Insurance: Group 17

Price
UK market price for the standard car (including VAT) in February 1999 was £20,950.
Included in the basic price is a one-year free recovery membership of the Automobile Association and each car comes with a one-year unlimited mileage warranty and an eight-year warranty against perforation for the unique aluminium chassis unit.

Optional Extras

Metallic paint	£690
Radio fitting kit	£150
Leather trim seats	£585
Driving lamps	£255
Hard top	Primer only £900 + VAT; painted black £1,050; dealers will paint to match car
Thatcam One approved Cobra alarm/immobilizer	£295

Specification of the 190 Elise (where different from the standard car)

Engine (190 VHPD)

Power	190bhp @ 7,000rpm
Max. torque	189Nm @ 5,600rpm

Engine specification developed by Rover for aftermarket applications, and also meets strict durability targets. Modifications consist of changes to cylinder head, valves, pistons, crankshaft and flywheel, and uses solid valve lifters in place of the standard items to give a maximum of 8,000rpm.

Competition Air Filter and Cold Air Box
Designed to fully optimize the 190 engine in the Elise. Manufactured from carbon fibre to reduce weight.

Close Ratio Gearbox
Changes to fifth gear and final drive ratio give improved vehicle performance.

First	2.2923
Second	1.75
Third	1.307
Fourth	1.033
Fifth	0.848
Final drive	4.2:1

Competition Dampers
Koni dampers with modified open and closed lengths, and incorporating an adjustable spring platform to reduce vehicle ride height. In addition, changes to internal bump and rebound damping valving provide improved track performance.

Competition Springs

Higher rate front (40N/mm) and rear (50N/mm) springs to improve track performance whilst still providing acceptable road comfort. These springs are designed to fit the competition dampers and lower the vehicle ride height.

Front Anti-Roll Bar

Fits original mountings and gives a higher rate with some provision for adjustment.

Competition Seats

Unique FIA-approved competition driver's seat to fit the Elise complete with mounting system and provision for six-point safety harness. Enables the driver to sit low in the vehicle.
Matching passenger seat has standard passenger seat shell, trimmed to colour-match competition seat. To be used with six-point safety harness.
Full FIA-approved six-point competition seat belts unique to the Elise are fitted.

Competition Silencer Kit

Enhances noise quality and reduces overall weight.

Catalyst Replacement Pipe

Straight pipe to replace catalyst for competition use.

Brakes

Cast iron brake discs for competition use with slick tyres. Direct replacement for standard disc to withstand higher temperatures.
The cast iron discs are fitted with competition pads.

Uniball Rear Toe Link Assembly

Direct replacement for current production assembly to cope with the increased loads associated with slick tyres.

Oil Cooler Kit

Oil cooler to reduce oil temperature during competition, especially in high ambient temperatures.

Fire Extinguisher

Both hand-held and plumbed-in systems available.

Competition Battery

Lightweight battery and mounting to fit standard vehicle. Battery master switch fitted for competition use.

Roll Cage

FIA-approved roll-over bar with diagonal bracing for circuit use, or smaller brace allowing passenger seat to be used.

Front and Rear Clamshells

Lightweight carbon-fibre front and rear clamshells for competition use to reduce overall vehicle weight.

Fuel Cap
Non-locking fuel cap.

Polycarbonate Rear Cabin Glass
Lightweight rear cabin glass.

Road Specification Tyres
Front, standard: 185/15 Pirelli P Zero
Rear, optional: 225/45/16 Pirelli P Zero

Lotus engineers clocked up countless miles at Nardo test track during the Elise's durability trials.

4 Chassis Design

The extrusions that go to make up the Elise chassis and the chassis itself are now made by Hydro Raufoss Automotive UK. It's probably best to outline the firm's ancestry here, so that the connection with the Danish Hydro company that originally made the chassis becomes clear. Its parent is the Norwegian Raufoss Automotive AS company, which was 20 per cent owned by Hydro from 1995 to 1997. In April 1997 Norsk Hydro acquired 100 per cent of Raufoss Automotive AS and formed a new division called Hydro Raufoss Automotive.

At the start of the project, Raufoss Automotive UK were asked by Lotus and the Danish Hydro Aluminium Automotive Structures to help with the engineering and supply of the 'non-chassis components'. These included the door beam assembly, door hinges, glass channel, dash panels, pedals and pedal box.

The UK firm had supplied Lotus for a number of years with the Elan header rail, which was made from a stretch-formed and machined aluminium extrusion. For the Elise project Raufoss Automotive UK were asked to supply more than thirty-five non-chassis components. In addition, the main chassis structural sidemember was designed to be stretch-bent. This was perhaps one of the greatest manufacturing challenges on the vehicle, as the sidemember has very thin walls and was designed to be a visible area, bringing cosmetics into the issue.

Raufoss Automotive UK were about the only place in the UK where the necessary skills and equipment were available to manufacture this vital chassis component.

Because of the pace of the project, the extrusions had already been tooled at Hydro Aluminium 5 plant at Tonder. So the logistics of the operation decreed that the sidemembers be extruded in Denmark, shipped to the UK and bent at Raufoss Automotive, then shipped back to Denmark. They were then anodized and built into the chassis, which was then shipped back to Lotus for assembly. According to Bob Mustard at Raufoss, this plan was fine for the original planned production of 750 units a year, but caused some headaches as the volume ramped up.

The company signed an agreement with Lotus to transfer the Elise chassis production to the UK in 1998. This would not be at the Bromyard plant but at a new factory in nearby Worcester, set up as a low-volume aluminium spaceframe facility to service the specialist UK manufacturers. It was designed from the outset as a 'clean facility', specifically to facilitate production

Lengths of extruded aluminium rest on the run-out table of the P-16 extrusion press at Hydro Aluminium's Tonder plant in Denmark.

of automotive structures utilizing bonding and mechanical fasteners rather than welding. It would provide the capacity and flexibility for the manufacture of a number of vehicle structures of various types, made alongside each other in a more economical fashion than was possible with a more traditional approach.

Hydro Raufoss Automotive UK obtain all the extrusions from elsewhere in the group. For example, the pedal extrusions come from the Hydro Aluminium Profiler at Karmoy on the west coast of Norway, while other extrusions come from Hydro Aluminium Alupress in South Wales. They then fabricate the parts by sawing, stretch-bending, machining, welding, pressing and punching the extrusions. Some are then powder-coated, anodized or painted before being supplied to Lotus.

Most of the Elise design was done in partnership with Hydro Aluminium Automotive Structures in Tonder (now known as Hydro Raufoss Automotive Tonder). Much of the credit for the original thought behind the detailed design of the aluminium parts goes to Peter Bullivant-Clark. He spent nearly two years working with Lotus on the project and introduced many of the Lotus engineers to the new way of thinking required to deliver an effective extruded aluminium design.

Everyone at Lotus acknowledges the huge contribution Peter made to the Elise being the success it is today. He encouraged Lotus engineers to 'think extrusion' and 'think bonding', and the rapport that developed in the Elise team between the aluminium expert and the vehicle design team was a major contributory factor in the success of the project.

Peter had worked on a number of vehicle development programmes prior to the Lotus project, and he brought much of his experience from those projects to the Elise

project. In the team at Lotus he found good engineers willing to tear up the rulebook and go back to basics to deliver a product designed and developed from scratch rather than evolved from a previous model.

Prior to this, Hydro had spent a number of years investigating the use of aluminium extrusions for vehicle spaceframes. In addition a considerable amount of basic research on – for example – joining techniques was carried out. There are just over a hundred people employed at Bromyard, of whom only five were working on Lotus components in mid-1998. Clearly this would escalate once the chassis manufacture began in earnest at Worcester. The factory floor space area is approximately 3500sq. m, plus offices and workshops.

In fact, Hydro Raufoss Automotive UK and their historic predecessors in Bromyard have manufactured aluminium components for about twenty-five years. They are suppliers solely to the automotive sector, and supplying bumper beams to Jaguar and Rover Group, as well as a variety of other components such as roof rails for Rover, sunroof components for Renault, and the sump-guard for the Land Rover Freelander.

RICHARD RACKHAM: THE ENGINEERING VIEW

Richard Rackham's first job at Lotus was in the late 1980s when the company was working on the ride and handling of the Isuzu Piazza – rather a forgotten car now – and he was brought in to do the design work on the modifications needed. John Miles was the development engineer at the time, and after one outing on the track with him, Richard realized that there are good drivers and there are mere mortals. He also worked in the handling department under Roger

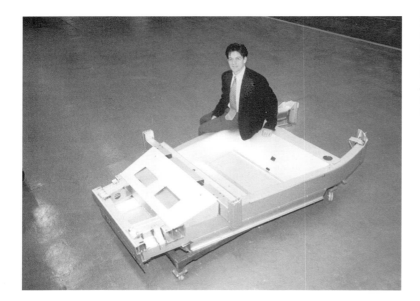

The Elise chassis was the inspiration of lead chassis design engineer Richard Rackham. It was originally made in Denmark by Hydro Aluminium, but production was subsequently transferred to Hydro Raufoss in Worcester.

Becker improving handling by engineering changes, and he also carried out much of the design work for the racing Esprits, including Le Mans 1993, after which he was involved in the Elise project. He told me:

> The Elise is basically a download on everything that I have learned about making normal road cars handle properly, and how to design racing cars. Basically I have made a racing platform with sufficient adjustments in it to make the most of its limitations as a road car. That's why its handling is so good: everything that needs to be tuneable can be tuned – but without upsetting other areas – and people like John Miles bring their own particular expertise to bear to refine it.

Before he came to Lotus, Richard worked for Aldridge Engineering Consultants in Long Stratton, Norfolk, on the design of a Formula First racing car. Geoff Aldridge started off designing F1 cars for Lotus, and the consultancy was a major supplier of expertise to Lotus. It was through this that

Richard landed a job there. Prior to that he spent three years designing special purpose machinery with Vickers Engineering in West London:

> That was like having the biggest Meccano set in the world; I think that put me into that way of thinking, and I use that in my work now. It's quite an evolutionary thing, and people do try to use evolution in car design. If it doesn't work, you have to change your thinking with the materials, and the process can be very long. The Elise has been revolutionary in that respect.
>
> It's not just car handling but all the other associated factors as well. We wanted it to be a car that you immediately feel at home with when you sit in it. That means creating the right environment.

Richard's involvement goes right back to the early design stages when Lotus set up the driving environment in a wooden box, set up with a steering wheel, gear lever and a seat that they could play around with it to get the right sort of driving environment.

The Elise comes in hues of all descriptions, and this silver car was shot by Tom Wood in the studios of the National Motor Museum at Beaulieu.

Only two car manufacturers have an automotive engineering consultancy: Porsche and Lotus. The Elise is the product of Lotus's engineering ingenuity and expertise.

The Elise is always a delight to drive, and the steering is amazingly direct, as well as being fingertip light. The smallest input makes for a change of direction.

The Elise is redolent of the sports racing cars that we used to drool over in the mid-1960s, and that's no wonder because many of designer Julian Thomson's influences came from that era. Thus, the Elise is a combination of flowing lines coupled with a hint of aggression, excitement, and a purposeful stance on the road.

Lotus development expert Dave Minter rolls the Elise Sport off the apron for a shakedown on the Hethel test track. By autumn 1998 Lotus had sold forty units of this model to competitors all over the world, including Australia and the USA.

An aerial view of an Elise Sport car, showing its racing seats, full harness belts, fire extinguisher and roll-over cage. Front and rear body panels are made of Kevlar and are considerably lighter than the standard clamshells.

The Elise Sport car is powered by a highly tuned version of the Rover K-series engine, and runs with lowered and modified suspension. This is Lotus's promotions car at speed on the Hethel test track.

The Lotus Elise Trophy was introduced in Italy in 1997, and attracted the interest of many Italian drivers. The championship consisted of nine races, eight of which were in Italy and one at Rijeka in Croatia. There were two rounds each at Vallelunga, Magione, Misano, and Varano.

Gianni Giudici clips an apex in his Martini-sponsored Elise during a round of the Elise Trophy series at Vallelunga near Rome. Some Elise Trophy cars raced in the Six Hours of Vallelunga, where the first Elise finished fifth overall.

Alberto Pedemonte leads the pack at Rijeka, when the Elise Trophy ventured out of Italy for a round in Croatia on 20 July 1997.

The Elise is a car in the true Colin Chapman mould, and its design goes back to the core values of Lotus, which is all about achieving high performance through low mass.

Headlights and indicators are recessed in niches, while heat escapes from the radiator via the ducting in the front panel

This is the original 1995 Frankfurt Show car, distinguished by an absence of roll-hoop cover and lack of hood facilities, and it serves to demonstrate that subsequent production models differed very little from the original concept. This car was later sold to Zytec Engineering, who turned it into the first of their electric prototypes.

The five-spoke Elise wheels were designed in-house and made by Alloy Wheels International, and measure 5.5J x 15 front and 7J x 16 rear. They are shod with Pirelli P Zero tyres, 185/55 R15 at the front and 205/50 R16 at the rear.

The wheels are right out at the edge of the wheelarches so that the car sits squat on the road.

The cockpit of the Elise is a purposeful, no-nonsense environment, while the Lotus-designed aluminium filler cap provides something to polish.

The perspex headlight covers fitted on this early production model were intended to be cost-optional extras, but accuracy problems in their production process meant they were withheld pending a satisfactory solution. They were reinstated on the 111S model.

In detail, Elise styling is a subtle blend of inlets and outlets, of concave and convex curves.

Rear lights and indicators are housed individually below the spoiler, with reflectors set either side of cooling outlet.

Around 1,500 Lotuses arrived at Hethel from all over the world for the company's fiftieth anniversary celebrations in September 1998, and the whole spectrum of contemporary colour options was represented by the large Elise contingent. This metallic silver-grey car is fitted with the optional works hard-top.

Although Lotus may yet produce a coupé version of the Elise, possibly powered by the Rover KV6 engine, the closest owners can get to a closed car at present is to fit the optional GRP hardtop. From 1998 onwards – post VIN 3331 – it cost £900 in primer or £1,050 in black (plus VAT); alternatively, dealers would paint the top to match the colour of the car.

That was translated into the chassis of the real car to provide the fundamentals for the prototype Elise. Richard maintains, quite rightly, that the Elise is a different sort of car from the second-generation Elan, and is appreciated by a different sort of customer. The Elise is minimalist, a car for drivers.

It goes back to Chapman's principles in its concept, construction, light weight, which is why we don't need to have a great deal of power to make it a performance car. It is a very frugal car in terms of fuel and consumable items like tyres and brakes; the brakes last virtually indefinitely. You can run constantly over three days on a circuit and you won't need to replace any brake pads or discs.

There are half a dozen fundamental things on a car that need to be independently adjustable, and if you have those you can make the most of it, instead of having to make major compromises. Certain elements of the Esprit racing programme filtered down to the Elise, like stiffness, and the ability to adjust the cambers, which is the how the tyres lean, and also the sort of feeling you get in a race car, the directness of the gear shift and the steering ratios. Good racing cars have everything in just the right place – the relationship of the gear shift to the wheel, where the pedals are in relation to each other and the body and the seating position.

It was at this point that I suddenly remembered how the seat had been for me (*see* Chapter 6). It's all very well being able to pump up the backrest to adjust lumbar support, but as far as I'm concerned, there's not nearly enough meat in the seat below the thighs. It didn't hug me like I felt it ought to, and there was always scope for the backside to shift from side to side. By contrast I drove

to circuits all over the country in my Alfa GTV6 club racer, and always felt completely comfortable in a Sparco seat (admittedly personally customized with cavity insulation foam). So why can't the Elise be the same? Richard responded:

Sure, the seat is a compromise because obviously we wanted to keep the person as low as possible. From the compressed foam to the underside of the car is just less than 20mm. The floor itself is 1.5mm thick, the bottom of the seat is 3mm off the floor, the seat itself is about 2.5mm thick, and the compressed foam squabs are about 8mm, and that's it. All racing cars need a low centre of gravity, and that's why we've come down as low as possible. As to your sideways movement, the width of the seat, we designed it around the average person, and you are probably quite slim in the hips – I don't know – but clearly we have to go for Mr. Average.

I reflected for a moment on the Alpine A110 Berlinette, which ranks about number five on my list of all-time good-lookers (the Elise beats it), but when I once tried to sit in one, I found it virtually impossible to fit

The Elise is largely made up of parts manufactured in house, including the complete seat assembly. Here an operator applies the final trim stage.

into the bucket seat. In which case, Monsieur Average would rattle around like a legume in a pod in the Elise.

But Richard had another point to make:

The inside of the car is designed around the seating position, and the seat relates to where your hips are and where your legs go. We also need to keep an eye on the future, when we may be able to go into America, and at that point we have to design for an unseated, unbelted occupant. We refer then to where the knee is in relation to the dash, so that if you have an accident you go forward and your knee hits the dash and stops you submarining under the dash. So you see it's not just about comfort, it's about crash legislation in the future as well.

There are so many other things in the equation. When cars are crashed for the type approval test, they have the seats installed, and we nominate the point where the occupants' hips are in the car, and that's where the crash dummies are put in. The crash test dummies are a certain size, so the inside of the car is designed around these dimensions. Your car passes the test with what is deemed to be the average-sized person on board. In fact we only had to pass the 'Reg 12' trolley test, which is where you drive the car straight into a brick wall at 30mph (48km/h). The requirement for that is that the steering column doesn't move more than about 5in (125mm) in the horizontal or 5in up or down. That test was very good for the Elise. I think it moved about 20mm or 25mm in either direction, so we were well inside the limit and the car was virtually drivable after that. Most cars are completely destroyed.

There are about twenty fundamental tests involved in obtaining European type approval, and the Elise really only stumbled on one of them. This was all to do with the rake of the windscreen – Lotus couldn't square that with the required vision lines and wiped areas – so there had to be a significant rethink on the slope of the screen. They had to change the angle of rake and make it more upright to comply.

This was something that only became apparent after Lotus had built a prototype, and the methodology would be different

The windscreen's curvature and angle of rake caused numerous problems during the design stage. With the issue finally resolved, a screen is thoroughly cleaned and inspected before being bonded in place on the assembly line.

now. They would examine potential problem areas using computer-aided design before they actually made anything. However, because the Elise design programme was so short, and several aspects of it were running simultaneously, there were elements of the old-fashioned design process about it. Richard explained:

> For instance, we were recently working on the Esprit replacement and we would feed the relevant information about things like the sight-lines and wiped areas of the screen to Julian [Thomson], so that he didn't waste his time making models that didn't work. Although he still takes a little bit of licence, because if he made a scale model exactly the same size as the real thing it would look terrible. You have to apply some fudge factors in there.

I recalled that this is what the makers of scale models like Dinky Toys do, exaggerating some of the subject's prominent features to bring out its main characteristics. Richard confirmed:

> That's exactly what he does. So you can tell him what the reality is and he will interpret it into a scale model, to give the right impression of what a real full sized car would look like. All these scale models are viewed at waist height, but you never see a real vehicle at waist height. It's on the floor, so you never see a full size vehicle like that. The part of a full-sized vehicle that catches your eye is all around the top of the door and anything at eye level.

Although Richard Rackham was responsible for the chassis design, his brief was to look at the Elise package as a whole.

> We began with a full-size sheet of plastic gridded paper, and we added the occupant,

the engine and the wheels, and filled it all up, and that was the packaging of the car, done in conjunction with Julian. Everything was kept as low and as forward as possible to improve the weight distribution. This package was transferred to the computer later in the programme by Dave Woods, who's another Lotus long-termer. The chassis actually filled the gaps. It's more than just a structure. It's part of the style of the car as well, because it's so visible in the design. It was approached in a way that doesn't generally happen within the automotive world. The chassis was designed to be something that is aesthetically pleasing, and I think that's probably why it's grabbing so much attention. It was intentional, a design philosophy that you see in other products. You know that our inspiration for the Elise came from the Ducati 916 motorbike.

Nothing surprising about that to a bike fan. Motorcycles, especially in the supersports category, are at the cutting edge in more ways than just searing performance. I recently wrote a book on the rebirth of Triumph motorcycles; Triumph's 1997 Daytona T595 and 1999 Sprint ST models

Russell Carr works on the full-size drawing of the original design. When Julian Thomson left to style VWs and Audis in Spain, Russell became head of Lotus Design.

99

exemplify this use of engineering in the styling of the machines. Richard continued:

> Everything we do has to be executed in a very special way, so that even underneath the car, in the footwell, everywhere you look, you should see evidence of aesthetic engineering. It's not the actual motorbike that's important here, it's the way the engineers executed its design, and I want to continue that within Lotus. The engineering itself is something we can do here – we can make things that are strong enough. But to be clever with a design, to get the added value of making something very desirable just through its form and the way it is shaped, is not at all common. People have tried catching up with us, for instance TVR use aluminium window knobs. Their interiors are quite innovative in the way they swoop and curve, and it's a refreshing use of traditional materials.

JOINING UP

Richard pointed out that although there have been rave reviews about the shape of the chassis, what hasn't been appreciated perhaps as much as it might have been is the joining technology.

> There is no industry standard for bonding aluminium. It doesn't exist. You can't go and buy it off the shelf, and when you start looking around, many companies will sell you an adhesive but they won't sell you the process. Neither will they sell you any guarantee, so that had to be driven completely from the ground up by Lotus. That process was carried out by Daryl Grieg, who's a very logical guy, and his assistant Kerry Osborne. They liaised a lot with Pete Bullivant-Clark at Hydro Aluminium, and developed the Lotus

system, which is the only system in production in the world. It is based around available technology with a certain amount of innovation. It's very complex, involving the selection and grade of pre-treated aluminium, the handling of it, and the special technique used to prepare the surfaces for anodizing. After bonding the sections are joined together with these simple Ejot rivets. Then samples are tested for corrosion, and there's durability testing. It's a very big chunk of the chassis story.

Richard was at pains to point out that three long-serving Lotus draughtsmen worked exceedingly hard on the Elise chassis. Known in the factory as the 'dinosaurs' because they are all in their fifties, they are Keith Lane, whose links go back to the F1 days of Jim Clark, Brian Blackman, who has great knowledge of all Lotus products and runs an Esprit himself, and Tony Messenger, who endured severe hair-loss as a result of the pressures of the project. The computer model was generated by Richard Lenthall, and was produced to assess structural requirements for passing crash tests, where he also worked closely with Daryl Grieg.

Although Lotus were clearly going out on a limb with a bonded chassis because it was largely unknown territory, there was a backstop position. Richard explained:

> The chassis was actually designed so that it could be welded together without the adhesive. This is simultaneous engineering, you know. We designed it in sections with very thin walls – about 2.5mm thick – and if you only stick them together they are very strong. But as you probably know, when you weld aluminium you mess the properties up, and it's suddenly half as strong because of the heat-affected zone. And the sections are only joined where the actual weld is,

whereas the bonded sections are joined over a complete area. So you've got all these material properties in very localized stress points. That's why they fail. So to get round that, you've got to start off with much thicker aluminium – about 6mm – and then weld it together. Then it has enough residual strength to last.

Richard highlighted this as the crucial difference between the Elise and its erstwhile competitor, the Renault Sport Spider.

This is what Renault did with the Sport Spider, and this why their chassis weighs twice as much as ours. So the only way you can save weight is to stick things together. If the breakthrough in the bonding of aluminium had not been made then, we would have simply extruded the chassis in a thicker gauge, where the welding was going to happen, as you can still make a member with thin walls on the side, say, and thick at the top where the weld is going to be. We could have done that with another set of extrusion tools and welded it together, so there was always a get-out. It was in the back of our minds if the bonding hadn't worked.

He went on to describe an obvious problem that a designer faces.

See, if you are designing something which hasn't been done before, you can be really struggling, and sticking things together like this was a different way of thinking. Designing with extrusions was entirely different, and for the first month I was a bit stuck, until suddenly it became more obvious what the value of the extrusion was.

I asked him what was the first thing that had turned him on to it.

Just before the start of the Elise programme we were asked by a major British car company to join them, as technology partners, in investigating making a car structure from extrusions. So we paid them a visit and we agreed that we were going to make some innovations and both parties would learn from it. Shortly after that BMW bought this company, and they decided that it wasn't good for Lotus to be in their back garden. We had been going to use this link to fund our own investigations for a new product and feed the results back into this other

Completed Elises – plus a couple of Esprits – await delivery in the dispatch bay. Just before the start of the Elise programme, Lotus was invited to participate in a joint venture by a major manufacturer to manufacture a car using extrusions.

company. But by that time we had realized that there was considerable value in extrusions, and we decided to continue with them. At the time the technical director was Hugh Kemp, and he saw that there was an opportunity for Lotus to use extrusions off the back of this liaison with the other company, and he set up this deal. So if anyone should be credited with the use of extrusions, it is him. Actually, a lot of people have looked at extrusions, but it's what you do with them that counts.

I asked how they actually arrived at the configuration of the Elise chassis.

Well, extrusions are straight things. That is how they are made, and you soon ascertain that any bend you put in them is going to cost money and time, so the idea was to make the chassis as straight as possible, and keep the lines all as straight as possible. The other important thing to bear in mind was bending stiffness, that is, torsional rigidity and crash-worthiness. If you put bends in something, the stress tries to buckle it at the bend, whereas if things are kept straight then they are not going to buckle. So due to the limitations of time within the programme, straight was going to be the desirable route. Secondly, as we were using the chassis as the interior of the car, we needed it to look good, and this would save trim weight too. Every time you stick a bend in a piece of metal you are going to damage the surface, so we didn't want visible bends inside the car.

So it really was a big design decision, given that we wanted straight lines, we had to determine whether we could run a straight chassis member up the side of the occupant. The occupant needed to be very low, so it couldn't go underneath him; it had to go beside him. This member also had to perform a side-impact function as well. We had this vision of the driver jumping into the tub of a racing car as well. They are not easy to get into, racing cars, and when you are in one you need to feel safe.

One aspect that we don't normally take much notice of in the UK is that we are in the minority when it comes to which side of the car we sit in to drive it. Richard had this to say.

The starting point of any car design is that first, you consider a left-hand-drive layout. Next, you take into account full back lock. That's where the tyre on the left-hand wheel is kicked fully to the left, and the space between that tyre and your clutch foot (in a left-hand drive car) is normally the thickness of a piece of steel sheet in a conventional car. But we had to get this member through there, and because we didn't understand too much at the time about the bonding area required, we selected a nominal 100mm. So that was the starting point. The radiator that we needed to package at the front of the car was designed for a future requirement of 200bhp, because that is what we saw the ceiling to be. The other ancillaries like the heater, battery and so on, all stacked up behind that in the crash structure. It worked with the driver's foot and the hip in that position, with the wheel and the width of the car, and we determined that we could in fact get a straight member through there. That's where this straightness sprang from. But then of course they had to curl round to the back to pick up the engine, so we had these two bends to introduce. We did consider stopping it all just behind the bulkhead and running a separate tubular frame, but at the time we went for this particular solution. The reason we would have stopped it there is because of the complexity of actually putting this bend in what became the biggest section in the car. We needed to bend, and the bending process is very tricky. Luckily Hydro have experience of designing bonding tooling, and we worked together on its design, on how to bend these big members, and the way it works is this. The aluminium is not tempered. It's in a soft condition. It's shipped over to England, where it's bent, and it's shipped back to Denmark where it's heat treated, then it's machined and put into the chassis. So this bending thing is a big problem. We had the logistics of it creating an added cost. [By the time you read this chassis production will be carried out in Worcester.]

The bending itself is pretty tricky. That needed this special bender – I think it's called a Cyril Bath stretch bender – which

The Elise chassis are now made by Hydro Raufoss Automotive UK, although, as seen here, they were originally produced by Hydro Aluminium in Denmark, computer programmed and assembled in a virtually clinical environment.

is a huge and complex machine. You stick this snake made of plastic segments up inside the extrusion, and then you grab hold of the length of extrusion and you stretch it and pull it round a former. The reason you stretch it is to take every fibre of material into yield so that there is no spring-back. The problem is that all extrusions have lots of tolerance criteria. There's one for the actual shape; if you want a rectangular section that could be slightly lozenged, so it is leaning over a small amount. And the straightness of the extrusion itself has got to have a tolerance on, the wall thickness has a tolerance on, and the actual overall dimensions – like 100mm-wide extrusions that could come out sometimes at 99mm or 101mm – need a 1 per cent tolerance. So you've got all these tolerances to think about. So when you put the snake up the middle to bend it around, that snake has to be designed around the worst case, otherwise you would never get it in. Sometimes it goes into one which is the big case and that doesn't support the inside like it is supposed to; overall it is a very complex problem bending complex extrusions. That's a reason not to do it, as you would have the same problem with every extrusion you tried to bend, although some of them are not as critical.

I reflected that must have been quite a big decision to get over, whether to actually go with it or not.

Well the original prototype didn't have the bend in. The extrusions were simply cut off and joined with plates in a cut-and-shut, and it was only when we went into production that we put the bend in. The bend is a very elegant solution but it has always been a contentious financial decision. So we put the side rails in that position and the side rails are the mainstay of the structure. They do so many jobs. The reason it is so lightweight and it seems such a simple little car is because of the multiplicity of function of many of the parts. If you can make one part that does three jobs then it is going to weigh less, and the chassis itself is providing a very stiff platform for the suspension loads to work through, which is a fundamental requirement. It provides this low-speed side impact protection as well, to a very high degree. If you have ever been in one of these [indicating picture of Caterham Seven] you will understand what it feels like not to have any side protection.

Too right, I thought. If I owned one of these cars I would have to have a huge Safety Devices cage around it like the racers do. Richard continued:

I've been in one, and I feel less safe in one of those than I do on a motorbike. But the Elise provides that side impact protection, and it also provides this feeling of being in the aluminium tub of a racing car. If you go and look at the old Group C cars in the Donington collection, you look inside and it's all aluminium, and we wanted that for the Elise. The other thing the chassis does is to connect you with the outside of the car. Sports cars should make you feel well connected with the outside world while you are driving. You should feel everything through the steering. Because of where we put the A-pillar, when you look out of the Elise you can actually see all the way round a corner. You would never get a situation in the Elise where you are looking round the A-pillar.

You can see chassis that's inside the car, and you also know that that chassis is on the outside of the car, so I think that also

This Caterham Seven is powered by the 1.4-litre version of the Rover K-Series engine, but its lack of side protection made Richard Rackham feel less safe than on a motorcycle.

has the effect of connecting you with the outside world. This is added value, because whenever you are in it, you are aware that not only have you got the design of a sports car, you are being reminded all the time of what this car is about. You can see the bodywork out of the front of the car, you can see where the corners are, and that's a constant reminder that you are in a sports car. Whereas you can jump into, dare I say it, the recent Elan, and you don't know that you're in a sports car, because of the design, the position of everything and the interior of the car. You can't see anything outside of the bodywork looking forward because it is all fallen away so quickly, and it's the same with the Alfa Spider. These are fundamental things about sports cars, you know. With the Elise, though, even before you start the engine you know you are in a sports car. And that sense of anticipation has already started as you approach the car, as you feel these things, little hints of the past triggering off memories of the cars you've seen as a kid. So you don't have to actually be driving it to think it is going to be wonderful because the perception is already there, and by the time you actually come up to the first corner, you think it's wonderful anyway. That's why we can get away with such a putrid engine note, but that's legislation for you.

I supposed that's how it has got to leave the factory, but once you have got it home you could fit Lotus's competition exhaust without compromising the warranty. A spell on the track with Dave Minter in the sport 190 Motorsport car was an aural treat as well as a full-on sensory onslaught in just about every other way. Richard said:

That system makes it noisy, and in the road car you think you are going faster, but not much really. Perception is all, though, isn't it? The reality doesn't come into it. It's what you think is happening that's the most important thing really. Top speed and all that stuff is largely irrelevant.

One can only agree with him. Having worked on one or two serious motoring magazines, I know how those figures are obtained at MIRA and Millbrook, and it's all about how ruthless and horrible you can be to the car. Richard agreed.

Yes, it's about destroying the car. It's pretty sad, but it's interesting what makes people buy things. The Elise is very special and I know that it's like no other car, because when it comes to being able to access the limits of handling, it can make people think they are good drivers. That's the good thing about it. It tells you what's going on all the time, and you can build up a really good relationship with it. It's not going to bite you; it's going to let you have fun. Feedback has been good too. It's been a pleasant surprise just how many enthusiasts there are, and the Elise has re-established what Lotus should be doing.

FOUR-SEATER

I asked Richard what he was working on now: a two-plus-two Elise chassis perhaps? His replay was predictably cagey: 'Well, there's a lot of things being looked at within the company, but for obvious reasons I can't say what.'

As it turned out, in late May 1998, Lotus scrapped plans for the glamorous K-series V6-powered Elise coupé, known in house as the M120, stating that the car had become too far removed from its core brand values. Despite its more powerful V6 engine, the coupé was originally conceived as a softer, more luxurious and drivable alternative to its wilder roadster sibling.

When the Elise concept was developed we expected it to appeal to real enthusiasts, but it was thought that maybe people would want a more watered-down version later on. We may still do an Elise coupé one day, but it will be simpler and a lot more fun.

The stillborn Elise coupé was to have included an extra 150mm in the wheelbase

105

to accommodate the Rover K V6 engine, and create space for a small luggage compartment behind the seats. To make access a little easier, the Elise's chassis side rails were to have been lower, but the new roof structure would have compensated for any loss in overall stiffness, which if anything would have been marginally higher than in the roadster. Creature comforts extending to electric windows and air conditioning were also going to be included in the spec.

The coupé's rear clamshell was also extended by 2¾in (70mm), to provide more boot space and to accommodate its wider rear wheels more elegantly. The body panels featured extra cut lines and creases to aid an injection moulding process suitable for an annual production volume of about 3,000 units. It was anticipated that the coupé would have been marketed at around £30–40,000.

Meanwhile the success of the standard Elise had a knock-on effect on the Esprit. The supercar had been suffering the indignities of superannuation, with dealers clamouring for more luxury and equipment every year. The arrival of the stripped-down and more competitively priced GT V8 saw Esprit registrations rise an amazing 103 per cent in the first quarter of 1998, and the model seemed likely to live on for some years, as the increasingly focused Lotus company ponders its replacement. Richard commented:

> Obviously everybody's looking for a replacement to the Esprit, but as to what form it will take I cannot say, but by the time this book is done I suppose there might be something more definite. But you see what we have identified is a way to make vehicles. The way the Elise is made is unique and it is designed so that it could be assembled and serviced easily.

This is his impression of a visit to the Hydro Aluminium plant.

> The Elise chassis was made at the same place as the Renault Sport Spider chassis. You would walk in at one end of the factory, and the noise intensity would increase as you went along. And there were sub-assemblies everywhere for the Renault Spider, with people hammering

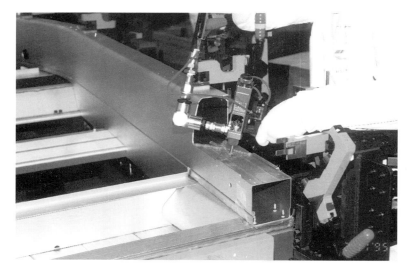

A gloved technician triggers a dispenser to distribute a specially formulated adhesive in an X-pattern to bond the Elise chassis components. The operation takes place under surgical conditions in a climatically controlled room.

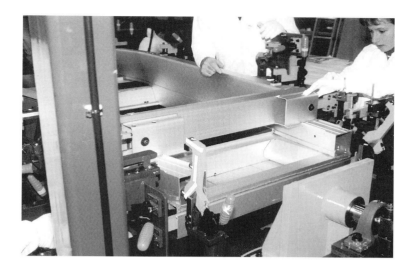

Chassis components are assembled in a jig, and after the adhesive is applied the bonded sections are secured with Ejot fasteners. The jigs are then placed in an oven to cure for 40 minutes at temperatures that do not distort the aluminium.

and banging, and welding sparks everywhere. It was just like a normal fabrication shop, with lots of muck and dust. Then you'd go further down and you'd reach a glass partition and you could see people inside, and it was like something from The X-Files. A complete contrast with the Renault line. You know,

everyone with gloves on, like they had found an alien or something. This was a climatically controlled room too, because with the bonding process you mustn't have any contaminants on the surfaces. The people in there were taking one car kit's worth of aluminium components from a box, individually wrapped, and the

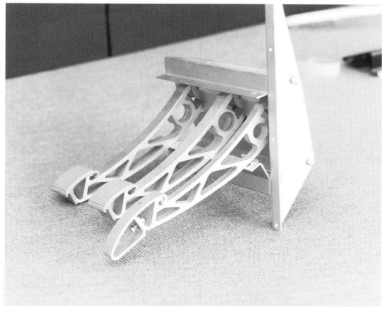

Detailed extrusions like the pedals and pedal box are beautifully neat. All the pedals have the same extrusion, the one for the accelerator simply being cut thinner.

adhesive was applied. They were assembled in a jig, with rivets, and it was all dead quiet. When they'd finished it, it went into the oven in the jig, so it was a much cleaner, nicer environment. Of course, those components had been through a machine shop, to be cut to length and so on, just like the Renault.

The curing process is about 40 minutes. The wonderful thing about bonding things together is that the strength is retained in the material. The temperature you need to bond things together doesn't degrade the material. And because the heat isn't localised like a weld, there is no distortion. You put it all together in a jig and you put it in the oven, and when it comes out it is exactly the same shape. When you weld things together they twist and buckle, but we end up with something that's incredibly accurate.

If you want every car that comes off the line to handle really well, then you need to control the location of the suspension pivots on every car. The more control you can have over that, the higher state of tune you can take the suspensions to, because there will be less tolerance corruption. So that meant that John's [Miles] job was made easier because each platform was always the same. If you take a regular production car the parts are all over the place and you have to make the worst and the best conditions work. But because the difference between the worst and the best on the Elise is so small you can get more from it. And that carries over to anything that comes on to this main structure: with all the body panels, anything that bolts onto them, the production process is much easier because the datum – which is the chassis – is so much better controlled.

That is where our major advantage lies, and we can use that. It's a big leap in niche vehicle design – say fewer than 5,000 units per year – and we can use that type of technology to do any sort of thing. We can do off-roaders, people carriers, as well as sports cars. There's a low investment cost, because the cost of extrusion tooling is very low, and the higher the accuracy, the higher the value, so hopefully you will see Lotus design associated with other car manufacturers in a similar type of structure.

The other thing of course is the suspension uprights. They also show how extrusions can be used, and that is the added value thing as well. The pedal is the best thing I have ever designed. It not only looks wonderful but it is very functional. Extrusions are cheaper too: that pedal costs £4, whereas the steel one for the Esprit is £10. So it has cost us virtually nothing and it answers all the requirements of the design. The pedal arm is one bit, and the foot pad is another, which is bonded onto it.

I asked about the rear subframe, which had to be redesigned because at Millbrook cracks were appearing on the original prototype. Richard immediately explained.

Well, I'll tell you the true story about that now. The original requirement was to design the complete car from extrusions, and it became apparent that it would be very difficult to make the rear subframe work as an extrusion. We needed a separate subframe because we needed flexibility for engine changes in the future; we needed crash-reparability so that if you damaged the rear subframe you could just replace it. So it ended up being a thing that needed to bolt onto the main structure, it needed to have the suspension bolted to it, and it needed to support the engine steady brackets. And every time you hang something on it, you need to reinforce that part of the extrusion, like this area round the front suspension, where there are little black reinforcements in the chassis to spread the load out.

We ended up with this thing that was covered in reinforcements, and extrusions were not the right medium to use. I said, 'Look, this is the wrong way to go,' but we had to go through the loop to satisfy ourselves internally. Before we went out to Millbrook, I saw Tony Shute, among others, and said, 'This is going to fail, shall we make a steel one as well? Because if it fails there we can just bolt on the steel one and we can continue with the durability test.' He said, 'No, we haven't enough time.' so it went off, and it failed because it wasn't the right medium – it was right to design the rest of the structure in extrusions, but not the subframe. So we came back and made the steel one. It was no surprise to me. There's the heat factor as well, because the catalyst is in the back there, which runs at 600°C surface temperature, and the adhesive used on the subframe would go soft at that temperature. We had to put a lot of heat shielding there in any case.

We went straight through the pavé [cobbled road] cycle with only small cracks appearing round the steering rack mount. If you look inside the footwell there are black U-shape brackets that are stuck to the surface. They simply take the load out to the edges of the extrusion, and that was the only thing that came out of the 1,000 miles of pavé generally. The bonded joints worked really well.

It must have been very gratifying to have got it right first time, I said.

Well, some people would say that it is over engineered. I wonder what Mr Chapman

would have said about it. But we had to start somewhere, and we estimated 100cm² of bond areas as there was no latitude in the programme for the bonding to fail. As we didn't know enough about it at that stage, we had to go for a slightly comfortable design.

I asked him about the source for the epoxy adhesive provided by Ciba.

It's an off-the-shelf adhesive. It wasn't developed specially. It's been around for some time, used by Ford to bond oily steel together. The special thing is the way we pre-treat the aluminium, and the way we put the Ejot rivets in to hold it in place. In the event of a crash, they hold the joints together. They are right at the edges of the joints, because like any adhesive joint, when it starts to peel, it will suddenly go, but if you can hold those edges together then the peel isn't an issue.

BATTLE OF WIPERS

One or two aspects of the evolution of the Elise have passed into legend, such as the business of the Citroën AX wiper motor. I asked Richard to comment.

Well, it's a contentious issue, because within Lotus there are many departments. There's the body engineering department, and the chassis engineering department, which does the suspension bits, the monocoque structure that we'll call the chassis of the Elise. I have done this chassis work in other cars, and I would like to cross the boundaries into other areas. I believe that whole vehicle knowledge is the key to good design. But that didn't go down too well, because there was departmental demarcation then.

However, I was working closely with Julian, and I could see that the area around the screen was getting more and more affected by the body engineering department saying the screen could not be wiped by a single wiper. Not legally wiped at any rate. So there were two little wipers on there, and the car was losing its essence, and we would have to make the screen stand up even more, and I thought that couldn't be right. So I interfered, to be honest. They'd given up on this single-wiper system, but by changing the angle of the spindle, I made it work.

If you take the screen, and stand the spindle at 90 degrees to it, when you get to the edges of the screen then you need more wrap. The spindle needs to lie down at a different angle round the edges of the screen and then come and stand up again. So basically I took the angle requirement at the full extreme and at the halfway house, and tilted the spindle to be half-way in between those things; this ensures that the pressure on the screen is better maintained. It meant shifting the axis of the wiper spindle, which enabled the wiper system's pressure to be adequate to wipe the screen. A lot of the design work then was being done manually, being drawn out, but I could see what needed to be done. So I built it up on a buck, tweaked the spindle, sprayed on a little water and it was done.

Any complicated design is dead easy, but a simple design is very difficult. The simple solution is the most difficult one to find. When you look at the Elise, it is a very simple thing, and that can be

Once the front clamshell is fitted, the body assembly is complete. Had the door-less 'step-in car' concept been carried through, the Elise would have been lighter and cheaper to make, but safety considerations made doors imperative.

misinterpreted, as it certainly wasn't easy to reach a simple solution. But it is worth it when you get there. And when you think of the styling implication of two wipers, the car would look quite different, for if you put two wipers on they would be offset to one side, and there would be extra weight and extra cost. You have this single, fundamental vision of what the finished product needs to look like, and you only let go of that as a last resort, I believe.

I prompted him to return to the early days of the project, when it wasn't going to have doors at all, and you just stepped over the sill, like a Caterham but without the side screens. Clearly the eventual solution disappointed him.

Yes, that was the idea, because it would have been lighter and cheaper to make. Doors are very difficult, we know from experience, but the difficulty was to do with the legal height requirement for the step-over distance. You would have had to have a running board, and the styling couldn't be made to work. But we were going away from that, because it became more and more apparent that this should be a car that you could lock up, that would be waterproof. And although this was supposed to be the modern day interpretation of the Seven, I could never come to terms with that because the Seven doesn't have the level of security and water tightness that a modern vehicle requires. So the Elise ended up with doors. We were disappointed that the doors were conventional. Julian and I wanted the doors to open upwards, like on a McLaren, but the body engineering department told us that was impossible.

At this point we referred to a number of Burago models in a display case.

The door could have been hinged along the top like a GT40's gullwing, or we could have still hinged it down in the conventional place and made them open up in this fancy way, like the scissor-doors on the Bugatti. But what I call a 'sciss-wing' on the McLaren, a combination of the two, is the best solution. That is something that I would certainly look at in future work, because I think the added value of doors like that is huge. But we were told it was impossible, so we didn't have that.

I suggested that fancy door hinges implied that it would be a coupé rather than a sports car or a coupé with a lift-out top. 'No,' he said, 'you could still have a conventional lid, everything would be the same. All the hinge actions could be down in the bulkhead if required.'

SEVEN BORE

I wondered to what extent the Seven had influenced them, which after all was a Lotus for its first sixteen years. Richard explained:

We bought a Caterham and pulled it apart at the beginning of the project, stripped it down and weighed everything, and used it, not as a target or a benchmark particularly, but to push the idea of light weight in the company. But we were never going to get as light as that. Some people thought we should but it was just a physical impossibility. You can't build something that is ten times as stiff and ten times as safe, and much more spacious inside, yet weighs less.

The C21 [Caterham] is a case in point. It's bound to weigh more than the standard

Rendering by Russell Carr of the Elise-based 340R prototype of 1998, displaying certain minimalist cues of the Seven as well as futuristic aerodynamics.

Seven with all that extra tubing and creature comforts. And yet – I don't know if you've sat in one – but there's nowhere for your feet to go! That's why the Elise footwell is such a great layout for a sports car, being so usable, and that came from the Esprit being not so good. It seems the perceived best-handling cars are the ones that are the easiest to drive, as well as being the best handling. If you're a great driver then you can stand more discomfort, but if you're not such a good driver, you need those things taken away, like getting your feet crossed up. Then bad drivers can access other parts of the car, but if they are in there not feeling too good anyway, they're not going to be comfortable enough to explore!

Safety was very much on my mind when designing the Elise, above and beyond the normal legislative requirements. That was for two reasons. Firstly, just prior to the start of the Elise programme I had lost a very close friend following a simple accident in a poorly designed car. And secondly, I had my own incident coming to work one morning, having been out the previous night with Dave Minter in the Elise. This wasn't the first run – not the Christmas run, which was Tony Shute and me. That was magic. But subsequent to that I was out in the New Year with Dave Minter, playing on the test track. And I got home quite late at night and was full of it because we had had so much fun.

The next morning I was telling my wife Rebecca about how we could slide it about, and she said, 'I don't know, people like you should know better. You're making a car that's dangerous, and it is just going to encourage people to drive beyond their limits.' I told her, 'you don't know where this is coming from. This car tells you when you get near the limit,' but it fell on stony ground.

Now at the time I was driving an Alfa Spider, a classic model that I'd bought new in Belgium in 1988, and I loved that car because I love convertibles. It has got all those sports car things about it, you can see the shape of it and it sounds good. So I'm driving to work in the Alfa first thing in the morning, and I'm thinking, she just doesn't understand. And I was driving along this twisty little country road, and I was being over-zealous and suddenly the car went, and I spun round and ended up facing the wrong way up the bank. There was a drainage gully in the bank like you get every so often in country roads, and the car dipped into this, and bounced me up onto the verge. But if that hadn't been there I would have flipped without a doubt, and the Alfa has no roll-over protection. And there were trees on either side as well, which I somehow managed to miss, and there had been no traffic. I just felt so lucky that I got away with that, and it made me more aware of safety in sports cars.

That is one reason why the Elise is a very safe sports car from all angles; the original car didn't have the composite front end on, and we didn't have a very substantial roll-over bar. There was always going to be one, but we ended up with one in steel, RAC-approved for racing, with a small modification. It's also got a rear impact structure, and we've had a few customers who've had big accidents in them, and they send in photographs, and say, 'here is my car, it is a complete write-off, and thank you, because I stepped out of it.'

The windscreen hoop doesn't really need to serve as roll-over protection because it has a very substantial roll-over bar. If you draw a straight line between the front of the car and the roll-over bar, your head is back within the confines of the bar. People have rolled these cars and walked away from them. If you didn't have the roll-over bar it would be a different story. But because it is there and you sit so close to it, you have always got this big hoop back there above your head, and the screen hoop isn't really relevant. That could drop down a bit because you've always got the front of the bodywork to take it. But it's lighter and stiff enough the way it is.

I pointed out that TVR, in their Tasmin series 'wedge' era, promoted that very raked windscreen hoop as some sort of roll-over protection, because it came right back over the cockpit. Richard pointed out the flaw.

Ah, but the bigger the rake, the harder it is to make work, so I doubt that it actually provides protection. The requirements for roll-over protection are pretty lax anyway. If you push on the screen surround with one and a half times the vehicle weight, and if it moves more than 5in (125mm), you have failed. The other option is you can just gently invert the car, so there is no dynamic roll-over; they do not actually roll a car over at speed, which in reality is when it always happens. The legislation isn't very strict at the moment, but maybe it will be in a few years. We will be well placed if it should happen, I'm sure.

The roll-over bar does lots of things. It looks substantial and it's part of the style.

I know it's covered now; you can see the cover is on, which enables you to take the rear screen out. Paradoxically, you would only remove the rear screen for winter motoring, because heat from the engine, not fumes, but heat, through some aerodynamic quirk, comes forward and warms up the interior, which is fantastic. But in the summer you don't want that, so you leave the rear screen in. And it really works well. The cover is simple to remove, with two clips on the inside; when you buy the hard-top, that uses the same two clips to hold it, and you simply have to remove the rear screen, drop the hard-top on and clip it all back together again. You can stow the screen behind the seats.

Richard took me onto the assembly line and talked through the chassis construction.

As a result of the pavé testing we had to modify the steering rack mounts to spread the load. But that was the only part we had to add to this chassis, apart from some little reinforcements at a suspension pivot. There are so many subtleties to the design. For instance, look at the way the steering rack's mounted on the same extrusion as the wishbone, which means you control the bump steer very accurately. It is very important to get this repeatability.

It seemed a good point to mention the recall in mid-1998 that centred on rear suspension bolts coming loose. Richard was rather dismissive of the issue and the swift

After the cars have completed a few laps of the test track they undergo a final inspection. Up on the ramps the flat diffuser panels and suspension can be checked.

The galvanized rear subframe is assembled to the chassis, and wishbones are attached prior to the fitment of the engine.

blaze of adverse publicity that the recall caused, drawing an amusing analogy:

> The higher the monkey climbs the tree, the more people see its backside. The Elise has had so much good publicity that the press were quick to pick up on the issue, but it was all a bit of a storm in a teacup really. We found that bolts had come loose on two or three cars, so we requested that owners get their cars checked. Some owners love that sort of thing, as it's an excuse for driving back to the factory to get the car checked over and having a look round. People who buy the Elise can live with this sort of thing. It's a bit like having a beautiful girlfriend who snaps at you once in a while. My Ducati has been recalled twice.

SEAL TRIP

Richard had more important things to say regarding the construction and bonding process.

> The adhesive is used as a sealant as well, and the way we make the joint is another interesting thing. You put a cross of adhesive on two surfaces, and when you bring the two halves together, the middles touch first and just squeezes all the adhesive out, so you end up with total coverage. When you can see adhesive round all the edges of the joints, you know those are totally made. So what you might think is a mess of over-spilled glue – really, if we don't see it, we worry. Also, there

mustn't be any air gaps in there because if water goes in and freezes the peel force will separate the joint.

Quality control is carried out throughout in the process. We do rudimentary checks when the panels arrive, and the guys on the line are onto it pretty sharpish if they see anything untoward. But they shouldn't get this far if there is anything wrong. The body sits on this little flange. The body side comes in, hooks into the feature on the extrusion, we stick adhesive on the top of that flange, and the adhesive on the body comes in over the top of it.

This hub carrier is an extrusion. It's the same grade material, but differently treated; and unlike the chassis, this is natural finish. There is another extrusion for the front upright. This hub is the same on all four corners, and it's off a Metro actually. The same ball joints are used at the ends of all eight wishbones, and the same inner pivot bushes are used everywhere. This way we can get economies of scale. The rear subframe we were talking about was made in house, and that is another good thing about it, because it kept a lot of people going internally. We make the wishbones in house as well as the subframe. You'll notice it's heavily perforated; the design is such that when we hot-dip galvanize it, which is how it's finished, the metal obviously gets very hot, and if you don't have all these holes in it, the sheet material buckles. So the perforations enable it to grow and then shrink again without losing its shape, so it can hold very accurate hard points, which is very important for consistent handling.

Richard is justifiably proud of the detailed extrusions like the pedals and pedal box because they are beautifully neat.

The pedals have the same extrusion for the accelerator, the brake and the clutch. They're just sawn off a bit thinner for the accelerator. The pedal box is just an extrusion as well. The discs [fitted on the SE model] are made of a mixture of aluminium and silicon carbide, though as you know, discs are normally made of cast iron. These are made of a metal matrix composite, so they are a third of the weight of cast iron. They're a lifetime component. The pad puts a layer down on the disc and then wears on itself. You replace the pads but not the discs. The discs will never go rusty. This is another thing from motorbike styling: motorbike brakes always look good and we wanted this on the car, so we designed our own calliper. AP Racing make the callipers. This disc not only looks good forever, but as it's so light the unsprung weight and rotational inertia are less. It shifts heat four times as quickly as cast iron as well.

So there are pretty impressive brakes in the car, and you've probably experienced that. We can also open the wheel design right up. We can make it very spindly to show the discs and callipers off better. But the weight difference is the big thing; the discs are more expensive at the moment but they will become cheaper. Lanxide in the States originally made the discs, but they are now made by Brembo in Italy. Lanxide are really metallurgists. This is the first application of metal matrix discs on a production car, but they are big in tube trains. They will reduce the weight of a train by about ten tons.

We moved on down the line.

The heater is an in-house design. We just swap the heater components over for the left-hand drive. We assemble the heater here; we just buy the matrix and the fan.

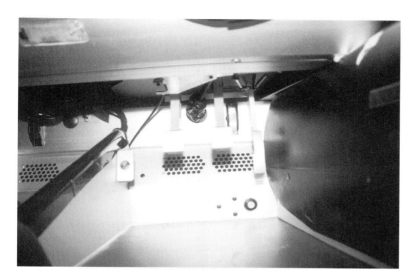

The bare aluminium of the footwell and pedal box is as stark and purposeful as in any competition car.

An example of using one part to do many jobs is the front crash structure. It has been stuck on at this stage, and you can see the bonding surface, which is stuck on with the regular polyurethane adhesive that is used to stick windscreens in. It takes the air in the front and it comes up through the radiator for cooling. These are the impact sections, which in a crash will absorb the energy, and those little ones in the middle are a token gesture for the pole impact. And out here is the support for the body. We could tune the structure during crash testing, laying up the different thicknesses of composite in different directions to change the pulse. It's a very tuneable way to make a crash structure.

Richard told me that composite crash structure design at Lotus was pioneered by Mike Tate, who was also responsible for the engineering of the soft-top and its composite members. 'He's a genius, and he's one of the few true all-rounders, just as happy designing planes or boats.'

The screen surround is not structural, and as a result is incredibly light. Richard rummaged around among the clamshells in a hands-on demonstration of their lightness and portability. It was the end of the day, so work had finished on the assembly line, although Radio One was still highly prominent over the speakers.

The concept of the design was to build the car with front and rear clam shells, because you can access everything on the car very easily by removing the front or rear bodywork. That makes servicing cheaper, repair much simpler and the build much quicker and easier. The rear screen will come out, and there are little clips inside. The same tooling is used for the indicators and rear stop lights. They're different colours, but the same shape. Thinking about these things helps makes the car affordable. Julian wanted something that wasn't off the shelf, he wanted a unique lens, and the only way we could do it was to house the lens in slightly different ways to make them look individual.

It has always bugged me that when you open a car door you always see nasty door hinges, but on the Elise they are extruded and very nice. There are some token polished bits as well, which is a reference to the Lotus 6, which had aluminium panels that you could polish. So the filler cap – a Lotus design – and the gear knob provide two bits to polish!

The door beam extrusion has given us absolute hell, because it is the only welded piece on the car made of aluminium. This is an extruded beam; that is the weld, and controlling that part is an absolute nightmare. These are made by Raufoss in Worcestershire, and they do the pedals and the side-rail bend as well. They have got the big bending machine there.

FLAT BOTTOM

We moved to the end of the line and into the workshops round the corner, and ducked under an Elise hoisted on one of the ramps to study its aerodynamic undertray.

The under-panel is a two-part thing. There are two NACA ducts. One takes air up into the sump and another one funnels it up to the gearbox. I wanted to continue the flatness all the way through to get as flat an undertray as possible, or else the volume of the air increases and drags the back of the car down. We were able to quantify that in the wind tunnel. I will attempt to put the flat underbody on to all the cars I work on, because of the aerodynamic advantage. That's the flattest underbody on any production car, and taking it right under the engine like this isn't normal.

I first saw a flat-bottomed car at Ronal wheels in Switzerland when I was working on the Lotus Omega, and I thought one day I might get a chance to do a flat-bottomed car. This was a Porsche 959, and it was up at an angle and looked great, so when the Elise happened, it was all flat!

The underbelly of the Elise demonstrates its drag reducing diffuser panels, which improve aerodynamic efficiency. According to chassis designer Richard Rackham, no other car has such a flat bottom.

Then I saw a Porsche 959 at the Silverstone Coys Festival, and I looked underneath and it was not that flat after all. It just gave a flat impression. But the Elise is dead flat, which is great for aerodynamics, because the air doesn't get all tangled up in the chassis ribs, exhaust and suspension systems that you normally find on the underside of a car. The rear diffuser gives you an extra 45lb (20kg) of downforce at 100mph (160km/h) on a flat road. When the underside of the car is flat, you also have much better perceived quality of ownership because you haven't got all those nooks and crannies filling up with debris and mud.

I wanted to clear up a long-standing issue about soft-top fixtures that had bothered me since I owned an Elan back in the mid-1970s, and this seemed an appropriate moment. What concerned me was the way you had to tuck the leading edge of the hood canopy into a lip along the front of the windscreen header. What used to happen above 80 or 90mph (130 or 145km/h) was that you would see a little half moon of daylight appear above the top of the windscreen, and the faster you went, the more the hood would part company with the header rail. If you went up to 110mph (177km/h), if you didn't back off, this half moon would get bigger and bigger until, bang, the entire hood would whiplash across the top of your head. And if it did that two or three times, it simply shredded itself. So I wondered whether this was likely to happen on the Elise. Richard reassured me:

> We were aware of that problem, because Tony Shute has a 1960s Elan and that's why the method was copied on the Elise. But it does work with just a bit of development. To make sure it's always kept under tension, the canvas is pulled tight from the back of the flying buttresses, so it is loaded all the time, whereas on the 1960s Elan it wasn't for some reason. It's inspired by women's underwear – the way it is pulled tight, like on the back of a bra. The original Elise hood wasn't pulled back tight. It fell vertically down the back of the roll-over bar, but looked weird.

I asked at what point this change happened.

That was another issue where we stuck our nose in where we shouldn't have, because the hood was a body part, of course. Tony had been working with the body department, and they came up with the original hood, but there was no way of fixing it to the roll-hoop, and we wanted to tension it downwards into the back of the car to keep it all tight. So Julian and I came up with this idea of pulling it back down to the buttresses. Originally we were going to have a rear window sewn into it, but that developed into a separate rear window. Obviously the original idea was the cheapest, but from the side view it looked terrible. It didn't flow. Normally a soft-top makes a car look very tall – look at the BMW Z3 and the Porsche Boxster – but when the Elise hood is up, it brings it down, flattens it off.

I first saw the idea of tensioning the hood rearward like that years ago on a concept car based on the Ford Focus, where the screen connected with two tails of the hood to the boot, and shutting the boot pulled it all tight. It was a nice system.

So the Elise hood was another one of those very contentious aspects, along with the door and the wiper, but that was what the programme was like. There was a lot of passion in there.

So presumably that also meant there were fallings out.

Oh yes, there was certainly friction. Julian fell out with the aerodynamicist, and obviously there were fallings out with the body engineers because I was sticking my nose in it. But we wanted the car to be as good as possible, and I was always supporting Julian's desires. He would normally get told 'no, you can't do that', and there would be nobody to try to make it happen. Whereas we spent a lot of time together and we would always be talking about the car. So it was a joint push, which worked very well. It's quite typical within car companies for the engineers to tell the stylists what they can or can't do, and invariably shatter their dreams. Whereas I was able to expand the style of the thing by the use of engineering, which was what we wanted to do with the car.

Was this a quantum leap towards the methodology for future projects, I wondered?

Well, we've been so close to the Elise, and I think we can see the way forward in other projects, expanding the technology, expanding the desirability, the accessibility of the product.

The Elise's gestation period was a turbulent time at Lotus. At one point, eleven directors were sacked in eighteen months. Somehow Lotus just seemed to survive, but the company has been a bit battle torn. For a long time we were funded by Bugatti, which went wrong because they were getting into trouble with their supercar, which wasn't selling, and that carried through to Lotus. Unlucky too, because although Proton are very enthusiastic about Lotus, making us feel quite confident about the future, they are no doubt suffering now due to events in the Far Eastern economy. But Lotus always seem to come out of it somehow, and certainly at the moment we've got a high presence because of the Elise. But I don't know what would have happened if the Elise hadn't been such a success. We wouldn't have attracted so much attention and so much business.

5 Shaping Up

JULIAN THOMSON: THE DESIGN VIEW

During the period when the Elise project was being formulated, nobody seemed to suffer more than its chief designer, Julian Thomson (head of design at Lotus until he left for VW in Spain in mid-1998), did.

> The skill of the designer is not only about how good his ideas are, but how tenacious he is at stopping the engineers from screwing up what he's done. Unless you've got good engineers, it's a constant battle. It's so demoralizing when people try and destroy what you've done.
>
> There are two breeds of people you have to deal with when you design a car. One lot wants to move the game forward and has got something to show, and the other group just wants to do their job in the safest possible way. Fortunately that group is in the minority at Lotus. You can get a lot of credit when one of these cars comes out, but there are those who don't want to take any risks, and have no enthusiasm for the product. So if you ask them how something is going to fit, how thick or how heavy it can be, they always take the safest option, and they won't put their reputation on the line. It normally results in a big, heavy, ugly solution. You always get, 'well we've never done it like that before,' which is pretty unpopular with us.

Thomson and Rackham are a polished double act, and you can see why they are not only close friends but were able to bounce ideas off one another when designing the car. Said Richard Rackham wryly, 'One of my favourite quotations is "beaten paths are for beaten men," and that has got me into a lot of trouble in the past! If you do what's been done before, but in a

Julian Thomson reflects. He remained firm when some of his ideas for the Elise styling were called into question by the chassis and body engineering departments. However, he was forced to redesign the rear of the car following wind tunnel tests.

slightly different way, that's evolution. But we want a revolution.'

'So who has taken the credit for inventing the Elise out of all the people you have talked to so far?' asked Julian.

'All of them!' joked Richard on my behalf. They then took it in turns to explain the history of the Elise design.

Julian: The whole idea behind the car as a lightweight Lotus, which could deliver more thrills, has to be credited to Colin Chapman. You can see a whole book full of them. It's just that we drifted away from them, and then we thought we should be doing what we've always done. So I think the Elise is a Colin Chapman car. But I don't think anyone can take the credit for coming up with the idea, because basically the Elise defines what a Lotus is. That's down to our founder, but the interpretation of it is down to people like Richard.

John: And yourself, for designing that particular body for it.

Julian: Yes, but there's more to it than that. When Bugatti bought us roughly four years ago, they threw a party and the site was open for everyone. We had a number of cars on display, and everyone could wander around. Giampaolo Benedini was put in charge of Lotus Design and Artioli had briefed him about future products, so he came down here, drew me apart from all the party-going and said, 'we must build this car'. We'd had lots of ideas pretty close to that before, but that was when the car took off. And what he said at that briefing was this car should be lightweight, back to basics, simple in philosophy to the Lotus Seven, and that was it.

When Bugatti bought us, Benedini was a director of Bugatti. He was the guy who helped design the Bugatti 110, and also the architect of the building. He was Artioli's product man, an architect and a big car fan. He had a lot of English cars, like a Lotus Cortina, Lotus 23, Jaguar E-type, and a Jaguar Mark II. He was a prominent historic racer; he was a big fan of Lotus. He wasn't based here; he just used to visit – that was when Bugatti were still running. But when he got involved in some of the nuts and bolts issues he was difficult, though he did have some good ideas. But the visits became more and more infrequent. They did come at the vital moment to sign off the car, though.

Richard: I can remember when they came to test drive the first Elises, and like all Italians he was immaculately dressed, and was wearing hundreds of pounds worth of shoes. Now the original Elise brake pad had a sharp edge on it, and he scraped his shoes on it, and we were told that we had to get rid of that sharpness.

Julian: One very intimidating thing for us in the design office was the fact that in Italy there are a lot of independent design companies, and most of them are only interested in designing prestigious cars to enhance their reputations. Mr Artioli had already been approached by Giugiaro, IDEA, and Gandini, who'd come forward offering solutions on how to design the Bugatti. And as soon as they heard about him taking over Lotus they reached fever pitch trying to get the contract to design the new Lotus. Artioli decided to give us a chance – along with eleven other design houses – to design the car. You didn't have any of this competition, Richard.

Richard: Well, to an extent I did. There were some people externally trying to get in on the Lotus chassis design. The people who had been involved with the Elan had moved on, and when they heard a new Lotus was coming along they put together a proposal that was fuelled by Peter

Stevens who designed the Elan. And he had got this team of guys, who he had worked closely with previously to work with him, and he came up with the style of car and they did the underpinnings. So they came knocking on the door saying, 'this is the way to do it', and I was saying, 'no, this is the way to do it', so there was some pressure about it. In fact I think their design was complete rubbish, you know – no side impact protection, expensive, low-tech, no passion about it. It was a revival of the front-engined Lotus Seven concept. But at the time they were thinking about their reputations.

Julian showed me all the other proposals from outside design houses for the Elise.

Julian: There were lots of drawings by different designers, all waiting to come in, and all done for free by the people who were keen to get the contract. We had been waiting around for years to design a new Lotus, and suddenly it looked as though it would be taken away from us. So that's the first pressure we had. In about February the following year, this 1m square box

arrived, full of all these drawings. And we had to put them up in this office and they covered all the walls, and Mr Benedini got the Lotus Board down and they had to decide which one they liked the best.

John: Had nobody seen the in-house ideas?

Julian: Benedini had been privy to our ideas at the time, and obviously by then we had had the support of Richard, and we had the chassis concept in some sort of form. Ours was by far and away the most progressive and the best solution.

I suggested that some of the renderings looked as if they had been done by schoolboys. Unfortunately, client confidentiality reared its head again and I was asked not to name them.

Julian: In fact there are some very well-known people here, and it was not a good way to start a project, being up against all of these big names. As design consultants, this is the backbone of what we do, but not to be designing your own product and potentially having some Italians taking over – it would have been the end of our

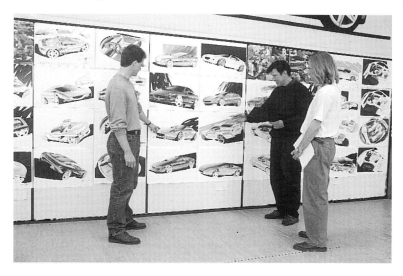

Before the Elise design was finalized, the Design studio was obliged by the management of the day to display a number of proposals from outside consultancies for consideration. Fortunately the Lotus directors liked the in-house design best.

123

business, frankly. We would have been shut down if we hadn't got this job.

We had to release a package to them. Even when we had designed our own vehicle package, we had to send it out to all our competitors. Bloody awful! No way to carry on at all.

Richard: When he first spoke to us, Benedini never specified whether it would have to be front- or rear-engined, or how big it was, if it had any doors or roof, how many seats, or anything. He just opened the door to a small lightweight sports car and he just said that they would pay and gave us permission to go ahead.

Julian: My opinion was that the company would have continued with front engine, rear drive.

Richard: The lightest solution is a rear engine – and the least risk. With no engine at the front, it's easier to make a car crash safely. We took the least risky route. But also, mid-engined cars are more racy. The mid-engine was becoming a key to Lotus imagery as well. It was seen as a Lotus cue – the Esprit was mid-engine, the Europa, the 23, all mid-engined, and the Elise just finished it off nicely. With the Elan, we were so constrained by the package of that car, with just one engine, it would have killed us off. We couldn't do anything with it. We wanted to change the engine, upgrade it, but we were just so limited by it being cab forward, front engine, front-wheel drive.

Richard: With the Elise we could try

The design started life in three dimensions as a buck made out of cardboard mounted on a wooden frame, which defined the position of the seats and the screen. The designers worked on the car from both ends and met up in the middle at the bulkhead.

another engine. With the GT1 chassis, we just extended the rails a bit and dropped the V8 engine in, and that shows the flexibility of the design. You can get more with a rear engine. And it is so much easier to style a rear-engined car as well, isn't it?

Julian: We tried to do a more modern version of the Seven. But it's like trying to do a new version of the Mini. People buy a car like the Caterham Seven because it's an icon, it's old fashioned, good fun, bumpy, a good laugh, and it's just a Lotus Seven, isn't it? And you don't go and buy someone else's Lotus Seven, and it was not regarded as being in keeping with the philosophy of Lotus to go back to such a retro theme, such an old-fashioned theme. We know how many buyers there are for Lotus Sevens, so there was no point in trying to steal those customers. We wanted more volume than that. So that decision was made quite easily. There was some debate about the size of the car. We thought about a really tiny little car, like a Cappuccino or Honda Beat-sized car, a Midget-sized car, but they look a bit too diddy, lacking presence, and the function of the car was obviously the overriding issue.

Richard: You can only go so low though, can't you?

Julian: Yeah, and the Elise is as low as you can get.

Richard: So if you make a smaller car, you only end up with something where the proportions are wrong for a sports car.

Julian: But the important thing to remember is that all those decisions governing the size and layout of the package that are given by the body engineering department are relevant to us. We talk about the styling, but my group is very much involved with the concept of the car. You find that all companies offering truly innovative products have to have a level of understanding between both groups. You can't just have engineers produce something, and then decorate it with different styles. They have to complement each other.

Richard: We had a wooden seating buck with mock-ups of the chassis defining the position of the seats and the screen, so we could work on the design of the car from both ends and meet in the middle of the bulkhead. There were so many decisions made, so many arbitrary, flimsy

A number of classic Lotus models were brought into the studio to accompany an early presentation of the Elise prototype, including an Elan, a Seven and a 23.

observations, that you have to move forward to where something feels OK. And as there were relatively few people involved it seemed OK to do that, whereas with a committee the project would never have shifted forwards at the same extent.

Julian showed me a picture of the early presentation of the Elise prototype.

We've got a variety of cars here like the 23, the Elan, the Seven, and this buck made out of cardboard; you can see the wooden frame of ours, and people sitting looking at the designs as if it were a competition. This is the image board we had of the car to show what we were trying to create. It contains a Ducati motorbike, a Rocket, a Lotus 23, all those kind of things. This car was really designed by a group of engineers as if they were doing it for themselves. It's the closest you could ever get to building your own car.

THE NAME GAME

I quizzed Julian about the naming of the car. Was it really named after Mr Artioli's granddaughter?

Yes. There were several names. Roger Becker's first project was called Step-In. Then it went to Club Sport for some reason, and then it became M1-11, and we stuck at that for ages. We even went to the extent of making up the decals and the badge design as 'One-Eleven'. It was very much at the eleventh hour that we decided to call it the Elise. And that was typical of how Artioli was. He used to visit as infrequently as every six months, and when he did come one day he said, 'well, we'll call it Elise!' And we said rather tamely, 'Oh, all right then,' and that's the

way it came to be called the Elise; Artioli's granddaughter was in there when we took the covers off at Frankfurt. At the time some people said 'Elise? Oh dear, how awful.' But we're all used to it now. It was going to be called all sorts of things. The Extreme was one possibility. It probably would have been called the One Eleven if it hadn't been called the Elise. And Elise is all right, I suppose.

In fact it wasn't quite as simple as Julian makes it sound. The name was finalized after a three-day board meeting, after which it had to be registered, which took several months. So although Artioli was definite about the name, it was by no means a snap decision. And in Artioli's defence, he was chairman and not managing director, and therefore not strictly bound to be on site that often. I am told he visited at least on a fortnightly basis until he moved to Norwich in 1996.

RETRO STYLE

Julian: The Elise was originally criticized for being too retro in terms of its styling. It came at a funny time in car design, when there was only one direction you were supposed to be going in. So first of all you had to be all sort of boxy and what we call in industrial design-type cars, 'functional' – solid shapes like the original Golf. Then you got the Sierra thing, going all blobby and jelly mould. Then you got the Audi thing, going all aero. Then cars were going a bit retro, like the Mazda Xedos, a bit like a classic Jaguar. And then much more retro prototypes appeared like the original Concept One Volkswagen Beetle, and the huge Chrysler Atlantic, which was an enormous American show car.

Then suddenly Fiat brought out the Alfa

One of Julian Thomson's favourite classic sports racers is the Lotus 23, introduced in 1962 and active throughout the latter part of that decade. It was campaigned with notable success by Jim Clark, Mike Beckwith and Trevor Taylor. Power units ranged from 1,097cc Ford-Cosworth to 1,594cc Lotus twin-cam.

GTV and Spider and the Fiat Barchetta very quickly after each other. And suddenly you shouldn't do retro any more; you should do really cutting edge stuff with no hint of what had gone before. Then Ford started 'New Edge' design, which was their way forward. And that had my designers really confused, because at that time you had to follow what was in vogue and there was only one way to design a car. But we stuck to our guns, and certainly the Italians wanted us to something which was linked in with past Lotus cues. And when the car came out, people thought it was retro, and some designers and some journalists said, 'Oh, you shouldn't be doing retro.' But it has been proved now that it was definitely the thing to do, and suddenly there is a resurgence into retro design and we are seeing it again: Alfa with the 156, BMW with the Z3, there's a new Mini coming out, and the new Beetle is in production. So suddenly it's OK to do that again.

When the brand is becoming more and more important, people are merely picking up the position we were in. We were in a position where people asked what our brand was about. The Elan had gone front-wheel drive and didn't look like any other Lotus before, while the Esprit had gone big-engined and luxurious, so people were really confused. And after the Elan we really had to tell them what Lotus was about, not only in the function of the product, but how it looked. It needed to have that familiarity; it needed to be recognized.

So that's why we went for this design. Some people think that it was a bit of a cheap shot, but we wanted a theme that had classical elements from Lotus. When Japanese companies are trying to steal your history or invent their own brands, like Mazda did with the Miata (MX-5), when they see the value of those things and they're trying to nick someone else's, the most important thing we've got is our name, our history and our heritage. That's got to be evident in the product, because that's what people are buying. That's what stops them buying a Miata or an MR2. They want to buy that Lotus badge, not just stuck on the front of the car. They want the way it looks and the way it functions. So we really had to be very strong in identifying the brand. That's why we made the decision to build retro at that time.

It definitely does hit the spot, and I think in the way it drives and the way it looks, it's designed to appeal to your most primitive urges. The way we're separating it from the competition is that it's more of a sports car than anyone else's, it's the enthusiasts' choice. There's got to be a real familiarity about it, it's got to be recognized, it's got to be really obvious.

You say it hits the spot, and I'm afraid there are a lot of blatant cues a designer can use on a car to really draw the punter in. So that's why you give it all those curvy flanks, it's got a nice view out, it's got big wheels, and people are going to want it. If you go into a bar to pick up a girl you don't look for an unusual looking one; you know what you want – and all the most popular women in time have always had the same features, haven't they? It is the same with sports cars. So we wanted to really play on that, and play on Lotus history, and really make it an honest product that would really charm people. We stuck it in the motor show at Frankfurt in 1995, and people instantly knew what it was about, they didn't have to ask what it was, it was so obvious. It is a back-to-basics Lotus. It is going to be reasonably priced and easily identified. They'd say, 'that's what I wanted' straight away.

I wanted to get Julian to reveal the styling influences that inspired him. I knew he had a 246 Dino, for example.

Yes, I have got a Ferrari Dino, and people say it looks like the Elise, and it does. But the Elise also looks like a lot of other cars. It looks like an era of cars. Richard and I chased the Mille Miglia one year, and we really love cars of that era: Jaguars,

Lotuses, Ferraris, and Alfa Romeos, all from that era. The 1960s was a passionate era for sports cars, a fantastic time, and that's where those cars come from. I can name some favourites: the Lotus 23, the original Ferrari 206 SP Dino.

But we are also trying to capture the feeling of some more contemporary products like Lancia Stratos and Ford GT40, to get a little bit of that aggression and a little bit of excitement in the car, a bit of that stance. Not so much directly in their features, but in the way those cars were stocky and sat on the road well. It's really that functional thing. With a sports car, if it is a Ferrari, and it costs a lot of money, you can afford to make it almost too pretty. But if you are pitching these cars at £20,000, they can fall into the hairdressers and secretaries bracket. It's very easy to get the wrong tag attached to those cars. It suddenly becomes a hairdressers' special, rather than a Lotus. You've got to offer that raw edge, and that is why you can't go too Ferrari Dino, you've got to offer a bit of GT40, a bit of Lancia Stratos, a little bit of aggression, and that is where we have tried to get with the Elise.

I wondered about the basis on which the Design studio works.

As with the rest of Lotus Engineering, the majority of our income is from consultancy work. The products we design for Lotus are done and processed as for a regular client. That's how we see it: it's a bit more ingrained than that, but that's the idea. At the moment we are doing quite a lot of work for companies in Asia.

I asked where Julian trained, and where he was before Lotus.

The renaissance of Triumph and Ducati motorcycles was achieved partly through projection of image, brand and character. In the same way that the Elise's chassis is fundamental to its styling, motorcycles like this Triumph T595 Daytona exemplify the use of chassis engineering in the machine's overall design.

Well, all the designers here have been to one or two colleges in the UK, either Coventry or the Royal College of Art, where I went about fourteen years ago. I was sponsored by Ford and worked for them for about a year and a half, and then I came up here and started Lotus design. It's been very, very interesting because Lotus is about engineering, and engineers have to grudgingly admit that the design and style of the car is important and they have to involve the designers. To actually produce a vehicle like the Elise, which is a

total concept right across the disciplines, requires that everyone understands everyone else. And it requires that the designers in my group are really diplomatic to make the engineers aware of the need for an aesthetic approach, a conceptual approach. But it's really more than aesthetics, it's really listening to the customer, knowing the market and what you are trying to sell. It is difficult to sell just the engineering of the car. It's a total thing. And so we've upset quite a few people over the years, I'm sure.

I think as a group Lotus is a lot more mature about design and product issues now than it used to be. It has even paved the way strategically to let Lotus go forward into the future. And we can come up with some really elegant solutions, and there is no reason why we can't put the Elise philosophy, how it was done and how the team worked, into something else again.

From the marketing point of view, Lotus has had a chequered career in terms of use of market and responding to the market. Colin Chapman never did any marketing or market research; he really just put his cars on the market, and because they were innovative, they sold. We don't want to get overly involved in marketing, market research, and clinics, that sort of stuff. That's a lot of hassle. But I think what is important is how you pitch your car in terms of its image, how you separate it, how you use a brand; I think that is where the Elan went wrong, because there is nothing unique about it, really. It just followed the pack. It didn't try to say it was a Lotus but tried to be all things to all people. The fact it was a Lotus and the fact that it was ultimately quicker from A to B than other sports cars of its cost weren't good enough.

The biggest lesson we learned in terms

To generate a degree of exclusivity for your model, you might have a waiting list like they do at Morgan.

of marketing and product positioning was from motorcycles. The fact is the European motor industry is just emerging from exactly the same kind of thing the motorcycle industry went through, the threat from the Far East and Japan. When Japanese cars came over and they were found to be reliable and cheap as well as well-equipped, Austin Rover tried to do the same, and they just failed. They didn't sell what was different or distinctive about British cars, and it is exactly the same problem that killed off the British motorcycle industry.

You've got to look at why the British motorcycle industry has risen again, why marques like Triumph, Harley-Davidson and Ducati have risen again. It is all about brand, all about character and all about image. Honda couldn't make a Ducati, not because they haven't got the ability, but because they need to feed this huge machine around the world that sells motor bikes to average people. So they've got to make these well-rounded, reliable sort of bikes. They've got to make lots of

different types. That's what they've got themselves into, and that's what Honda's about. But they've got the technology to make a Ducati – they could just go and copy one. Ducati, on the other hand, don't have to do that. They've just got to find some maniacs willing to shell out lots of money for something that looks gorgeous, could be unreliable, but goes like the clappers.

The luxury for us is that we don't have to find hundreds of thousands of customers, we only need to find a few thousand. And the product we do can be even stronger for those people. That's what we've done with the Elise: we've found a product that isn't for everyone but definitely is for some people. And those people would never be seen dead in an average sports car. That's our luxury.

SMALL-SCALE MARKETING

Before, we tried to do just what everyone else did, and we competed on their ground.

We can't do that because we haven't the economies of scale, the volumes we would have to produce, and we can't afford the labour costs. But we asked ourselves 'what can we do that they can't?'

We've got this fantastic name. We've only got to find maximum 5,000 customers a year, and we know there are nuts who'll put up with all sorts of things. And we can build our brand and make it stronger. We can do a total enthusiasts' car, we don't need to do electric windows or NVH, or worry about a walnut facia. We can get away with blue murder compared with the others and we can make a fantastic car that the enthusiasts are going to love. This will turn everything around.

And it's a fact that Harley-Davidson have done it as well; the interesting thing is that Harley-Davidson and Ducati have underestimated the size of those markets, the same as Lotus have. We've underestimated how many individuals there are. The car has been far more popular than I thought it ever would be. I thought the car would just do for a few nuts – I mean, I wouldn't drive it every day of the week, but it appears there are thousands of people who want to. It's incredible. I can't believe how many enthusiast types there are, who want to belong to these exclusive clubs and be part of this thing, and make a statement about being real car nuts, real petrol nuts. It's exactly what all the successful motorcycle brands have been doing, and it is working very well for us, and is something we can continue to push.

So that's as far as we go with marketing, and marketing on a small scale that Lotus can afford means, typically, identifying your customers and dragging them in and asking what they like about this car and what they don't. We like to think that the Elise has a bit of a Sony Walkman quality about it. There wasn't a customer base, because no one had a car like this. We didn't know where these people would come from. We couldn't go and drag a load

Without doubt one of the most attractive sports racing cars ever built, one of the works Ferrari 330 P4s leaves Mulsanne corner on its way to second place at Le Mans in 1967 in the hands of Mike Parkes/Ludovico Scarfiotti. For comparisons with the Elise, notice the ducting in the front air intake, the air scoops in the rear bodywork, and the lip on the trailing edge of the tail.

of Mazda customers off the street because they probably wouldn't be the right people. It's a truly innovative product, so we really couldn't do market research on it. What we could contemplate was what those niche-type manufacturers got involved with.

I put it to Julian that Lotus cultivate a degree of exclusivity about the car – they might have a waiting list, like they do at Morgan.

> Well, this is an interesting one, and I think when you're buying something which is basically an irrational decision, you're looking for a bit of security behind it, and the fact that there is a waiting list would seem to indicate that it has a strong value. I've done it myself when I've bought motorcycles. You think, well it won't arrive for another year so I'll put a deposit down on it, and then you've got a year to find the money, basically. But if someone came up to me in a showroom and said 'give me twelve grand and I'll have it for you next Tuesday,' I'd say 'woah, steady on!' It gives you a feeling of security knowing there is a demand for it. That is important, as long as the waiting list isn't too long. It's an old Ferrari trick, just limiting the supply of cars. Ferrari could make more. They did once start to make more, but soon saw the value of having a constant controlled demand.

DESIGN TEAM – DEVELOPMENT AND COMPROMISE

One aspect that Julian was particularly incensed about arose when the project was still in its infancy. The scale model was in the MIRA wind tunnel, and the aerodynamicist said they would have to restyle the whole of the back end. The original scale model didn't have a spoiler on the back.

> It is a route we're aware of. We always argue with the wind tunnel man, and we have a lot of respect for him as well, and he has respect for us and there is always a compromise. The designer wants to do the best possible job he can, as does the wind tunnel man.

But was there rather more of a compromise than he really would have liked to have made?

> No. That is a compromise situation, because he could have made that wing bigger and it would have worked better, and I could have made it smaller and it would have looked better. It's a genuine compromise and it's something I'm not too worried about. In retrospect, things like that give the car character, really.
>
> It comes back to this thing about not making it too much like an MGF, making it too pretty, and instead just adding a bit of function to it. We did design that wing initially, which was designed like a slash coming into the rear of the body, like on a Ferrari P4, and we felt that it complemented the ones in front. It gives the car a bit of an edge, a little bit of character. I was very upset at the time, but now it's just part of the car.

What about motivation, I wondered. Was there ever a problem?

> It's strange when you do a car like this. The clay model for the car was just over on my desk there, and the modelling plate is just over there. And I sat in front of the Elise being developed, and looked at it every day from 8 o'clock in the morning till 7 o'clock at night, for nine months. And

Following the initial renderings, the first scale model was made by Christmas 1993. It was finished in silver to one-third scale, and demonstrated the basic elements of the car. It is still kept in the studio.

you think, 'I'm going through a crisis. Is this what we need to be doing? Is this the right sort of car?' You get the car magazines every week and you see what everyone else is doing, and you think, 'am I doing the right sort of car?' And then you pull the covers off at the Frankfurt Motor Show, and you think, 'are people going to like it?' And you listen to every single thing they say, read every single magazine article. It's only about a year later that you can look at the car with any real objectivity and think, 'yes, I quite like it really.' It's only now that I've got over all the worry and hysteria, but I like it a lot now.

I moved on to ask Julian about the extent of his involvement with the Elise design. Did he design the wheels as well, I wondered?

Yes. But when I said I designed the car, it's not strictly true, of course, because I've got a big work force here and they've all done a little bit. Perhaps Andrew Hill, who is one of my senior designers, carries out the most stressful part of the design job, which is policing the engineers with regard to the designs. When we do a car we normally have an internal competition and get some scale models and some drawings and things like that. We all do a drawing of it, then we make some scale models, and my scale model is the one which went through and I oversaw my full size clay model.

But as I said, the really difficult bit is just maintaining that design and making

The second scale model was completed by March 1994. This green car was altered several times, but displayed much of the character of the ultimate design, including side air scoops, flying buttresses, top-exit radiator duct, and the headlights.

sure it's not cocked up, and that was handled by Andrew Hill. He probably put in a lot more hours than I've done. I did all the easy bits, but he did the tenacious bit, making sure the designers didn't mess anything up. Everything has to be battled with. The windscreen rake for instance, and the wiper. It's very thin between the top of the headlight and the top of the wing, and originally the engineers said it would need about 50mm of material. And they'd do a little drawing of that and we'd say 'no way', we aren't going to have that, it would look horrible. So they said, 'well, we can't do anything else', and Andy said, 'come on, you have to try something else.' And that happens everywhere, even down to where the front number plate goes. It's not a very practical place for it, and it'll get smashed quite easily, but it looks better there.

Here's another example. When the body panels are made, the moulds are oversize, and the body panels shrink a little bit – between 10 and 15 per cent – so the composite engineers said, 'just to be on the safe side we'll put in a 5mm safety margin.' But inevitably it's going to come out 5mm too big, and the wheels are going

to be buried inside the wheelarches. So we said, 'no, you don't want that. The wheels have got be right out at the edge of the wheelarches.' There's obviously a legal restriction about that, the tyre has to be covered up by the body, but we want to push it right out to the edge so the car sits squat on the road. And the engineers are saying, 'no, it's too risky because we may start manufacturing illegal cars.' Then we have to do tests, and we're pushing it all the time, and the engineers go on and on, saying, 'no, we don't want to do this, it's too risky.' But we've just got to keep ramming it down their throats, telling them they must do it. Andy Hill did that difficult part of the job, and he has got to take a lot of the credit for the design aspect of the car, because he was the one who had the arduous task of policing it.

We were helped a lot by Richard as well, as he was sympathetic to this car, exceptionally so, more so than any other engineer I've worked with. He understood what we were trying to achieve, and it's a good partnership. It's difficult to find engineers who really do have the same degree of enthusiasm. I don't mean that in a nasty way. Car designers are by nature

Most of the modellers were Lotus employees, and between four and six of them worked on the full-size clay at any one time. Here are two of them applying details in the design studio.

car enthusiasts; they're all young and they are car enthusiasts, and you can't expect engineers to share that enthusiasm.

I wanted to find out more about the nitty-gritty of actually producing the scale models and the original clay buck.

We milled a full-size model directly from the chosen scale proposal. It was the first time we had actually done a clay like that, and it's the way the whole industry works now, but it was fairly pioneering stuff then. Other people were not doing it regularly. As you've seen, we make scale models like this, and they are relatively quick to do. On the Elise project there are four or five versions, just so we could get as many ideas as possible; and when we pick

one we like, we cut it. But what you cut is only as good as what you have modelled in one-third scale. On this occasion, the one-third-scale model had too much artistic licence to it. I mean, the finished car is in there somewhere, but when we actually came to make the car, there wasn't a single part that stayed the same. Everything, absolutely everything, changed. The contours changed and the proportions and dimensions changed. You'd expect most of the skins to change subtly, but we changed the whole thing substantially.

To what extent does Julian have a hands-on role in making the scale model?

We do various sketches and full-sized drawings like those on the wall, which will

135

The original clay model, with only the nearside of the buck finished, stands at the factory in May 1994, when the design was signed off by the product committee.

have the bare bones like the engine and the occupants, and that gives the correct dimensions. And that gives the model makers a chance to make a clay model from these drawings. These are all on mirrors, as you can see, and the designer works from a clay model. Obviously the amount of information you can get from a drawing like that, and of sections through the car like that, is limited, so it very much a process of designers working with a model to generate the three-dimensional shape.

Lotus employs its own modellers, and there are ten on the staff.

The model makers refine the designs. For instance, if the engineers say there is too much curvature on the windscreen, then the model makers cut it out. The car is designed on a grid, and to make the clay, a piece of equipment moves along a track inside the plate and measures datum points and space. This data is fed back to the engineers so they can comment on aspects like where the headlight is relative to the ground. They measure it, and say,

'the headlight has got to be, say, 320mm above the ground at this point,' so this car becomes the master from which all the engineering data is taken.

I asked whether there is one particular model maker who needs to be credited for the Elise.

There were several model makers involved, but the two who saw the project all the way through were Roger Godfrey and Andrew Maclanacan (an Elise owner). Their skill is extremely important. There are a lot of very complicated shapes on the car, and Andrew did most of the back and Roger did most of the front. That is not normally how they work, but that is how it worked out on the Elise.

The Elise model took nine months. You can make a model like this in six weeks, but it depends on how much engineering you have to do; when you're doing a legal road car everything is done from scratch, and everything has to be in the right position. You've got to remember that a lot of that nine months would be spent making the clay model of the car, the

The Caterham C21 was styled by Iain Robertson and launched in 1994. The show car was clad in an aluminium body, although it was also available in GRP.

engineers designing the structure underneath it. And going off and crash-testing it and perhaps finding it's not good enough. Perhaps it needs to be two inches longer or shorter. You can imagine how long it takes to design something, crashing it and testing it, and coming back and saying, 'no, that needs to be different.' You haven't got a guy in there scraping this model constantly. Some areas will remain static while it gets tested or engineered or whatever.

Julian went on to talk about the GT1 sports racing car, designed by his replacement as chief designer, Russell Carr.

The racing car, as with all racing cars, is produced by people putting in hundreds of hours to build it and test it, and even then it's never really finished. Even when it is racing you're always changing it around. Like changing the aerodynamics, cooling – changing all sorts of things. There's not much left of the original road car. There's the cut-out round the headlights, the

On the stand at the Frankfurt launch in 1995 Richard Rackham (second from left) was buttonholed by the Renault Sport Spider's astonished project manager, who had been told that bonding aluminium chassis components was not possible. How wrong can you be?

Before starting a design, Lotus stylists prepare 'theme boards' comprising a montage of lifestyles and aspirations of potential customers to try to capture the ethos behind the car.

windscreen, the door from the original, although that's been modified. The rear quarters of the original Elise have been sliced through and more filler added in between to make it wider. Unfortunately it didn't win, though, and our bid to do a David and Goliath didn't come off.

But compared with Porsche, the race car must have been grossly under-funded.

We spent about a million in the first year of development, as opposed to £15m for Porsche. So it was a pretty valiant effort, but also the regulations were a bit strict. The organizers clamped down on turbos, because the Porsches were looking too fast, and they enforced more restrictions on the regulations. As a consequence, the Porsches were all very slow, and Lotus panicked and went for the normally aspirated 6.0-litre V8 engines; there was

These renderings done by Andy Hill in 1993 show what some of the original ideas were for the styling of the Elise. The front view has something of the stance of the Ford GT40 about it.

then more messing around with the regs, so there just wasn't enough time to develop it within budget. Which is a shame, but that's motor racing in this day and age.

THE OPPOSITION

What about the competition for the road-going Elise? The Caterham C21 and the Renault Sport Spider, for instance?

Richard: When the C21 first came out with the aluminium body, we were a bit twitchy about it to say the least.

Julian: But they've only sold sixteen to twenty cars. They deserve better than that. It just shows how loyal Caterham customers are to the Seven. The Renault Spider freaked us out, didn't it? We got a fax from *Autocar*. It was the day before the Geneva Show, and to Hydro's credit, they never let on that they were working on another car. Even though Richard was working very close to them, and they're doing this other car at the same time, they never let on. I don't know how they didn't let it slip. Their car came out and it looked extremely futuristic. Coming back to what I said before, we were looking for a design direction, whether to design a heritage related car. The Renault's a great-looking car. But I don't think we could have got away with something like that, because it wasn't in keeping with the image of Lotus. But it gave me the willies when it came out.

Richard: Well, again, the press were much more impressionable, and it had gone in the other direction. Interestingly, at the '96 Motor Show we turned up with the Spiderized version of the Elise, with the Lotus 23-style racing screen on it, and Renault turned up at that same show with a Spider with a full screen, windscreen wiper and heater, which was an Elise-ized version of their Spider.

When the Elise was unveiled at Frankfurt, there was an awful lot of interest, obviously. I was standing around near the chassis on the show stand and Julian was standing around near the car itself. And this guy turned up, aged about fifty or so, didn't introduce himself. And he said, 'How do you do this? What is this metal? How do you stick this?' It was like he was almost in shock. His name was Yves Legalle, and he was the project manager for the Renault Spider, and he claims that he wanted to stick aluminium together and the engineers at Renault had told him that it was impossible. And that was obviously the first he knew about it, poor bloke. We were feeling a bit bullish by the end of that, and we felt pretty good.

By January 1999 Alpine had stopped making Renault Sport Spiders at their Dieppe factory.

Julian: Well, to be fair, I don't think the Spider was meant to be a mass-produced car. It was a limited edition. Knowing how much it costs to develop a Renault, or a mainstream production car, I doubt very much if they made any money on it. It was a PR thing, and a very successful one as far as Renault Spider racing series goes.

Richard: They're a lot more expensive than the Elise, and I think they found they couldn't sell them. We've trebled our production – because we can – but I think if we hadn't been around, they might have made a big business out of the Spider.

DESIGNING THE ELISE

Image Boards

There's a lot more to designing cars than sitting down and doing a few sketches, and

The full-size model was built up on a framework of steel, wood and foam. It was milled to 40mm below the surface, with wooden pegs stuck in to the foam to 60mm as a guide. The modellers then applied clay to that depth for it to be copy-milled into the final clay buck.

going ahead with a scale model of the selected drawing. Lotus designers take a much more intellectual approach and think carefully about where the car is to be targeted. The market may be divided into three groups, and Lotus would be quite selective about the designs they placed into those groups so that they met the target specification, down to the type of person who would like one theme more than another. There's inevitably an element of guesswork and stereotyping in this, in deciding that someone who prefers one type of car would dress in a particular way, or wear a particular make of watch, but it's a way of establishing certain parameters.

So, before starting to design a car, the Lotus designers prepare theme boards in an attempt to capture the ethos behind the car, to summon up all the lifestyles and aspirations of its potential customers. These boards are each a montage of cars, motorcycles, aircraft, fashion wear, film stars and film adverts. The theme might be retro or futuristic, modern or minimalist, and the contents of the 'decoupage' or image board would reflect this. They would vary the approach to colour use as well. Particular colours and materials might epitomize the type of vehicle they are about to design. I was shown a number of examples, and cars featured in these theme boards included the E-type Jaguar, and the Aston Martin Vantage, while the motorcycle I spotted was – almost inevitably – a Ducati Monster. The James

Bond-type film-poster imagery thus created helps the designers get a better grasp of the essence of the car's appearance and the elements in the composition that go to make up the whole vehicle. Andrew Hill, the designer who was involved on the Elise project on a day-to-day basis explained:

> That way we can perhaps identify where the car might be going in terms of its marketplace and the types of people who would be interested in it. It's a way of explaining those ideas about the car's overall image to other people as much as to the studio. But industrial designers or stylists – whatever you want to call us – get a better feel for the car we've been asked to design. The Ducati, for example, is in there because its ethos and the way it's designed are similar to the way we wanted to approach the Elise. It's light weight, very purposeful, focused on a certain type of person, who perceives that the bike is all about the riding experience and isn't bothered about loads of trim on it. Whereas if you included the interior of an Escort, for example, you'd immediately know you were looking at a different type of person.

Lotus have also mapped out car segments in a demographic chart on the studio wall, with 'cheap' at the bottom, 'expensive' at the top, sports at the left, and 'grand touring' on the right. So clearly a Lotus would be on the far left and a Mercedes SL or an XK8 on the far right, with a McLaren F1 almost off the scale up at the top left. This chart is very much part of product- and consumer-related research, and where the car is placed relative to the points of the cross identifies its perceived market. Traditionally Lotus products are not aimed at the middle ground, which is the area of compromised touring car-based sports cars.

However, Andy admitted that these days the Esprit is moving back into the centre of the cross, and also getting higher up it as its price escalated with the V8 engine, although the GT3 was reverting back to the left.

'We should be looking to design something like the McLaren, but at an affordable price,' he said. 'Because we can.'

SCALE MODEL

The designers allowed six weeks to prepare their initial sketches, then made the first scale model, a silver car that was done basically to show what the basic elements of the car consisted of and what they might look like. It was one-third actual size, and done against a mirror so in fact it was only half a car. It was completed by Christmas 1993, and is still kept in the studio. A plaster cast was taken off the clay model, and then it was fashioned in fibreglass so that it was both light and durable. The original clay model was then modified to make the second one, and a fibreglass rendering created from that. This second evaluation of the project then led to the second scale model, which was completed by March 1994. This was a green car, which metamorphosed several times. In its final form this model contained some of the elements of the ultimate design, like the side air scoops, the flying buttresses and the top-exit radiator duct, the character of the headlights and the round indicators.

The armature on which the full-size model was built consisted of a very stiff steel framework underneath, which was loaded up with wood and blue foam. It was then dispatched to MGA, who milled it to 40mm below the surface, then sent it back to Lotus with wooden pegs stuck in to the foam to 60mm – looking much like a giant

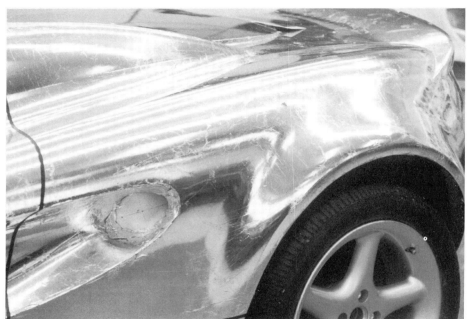

The clay model looks dull in plain terracotta, but the designers cover it with a kind of silver foil in order to reveal the highlights of the shape.

The wooden mock-up interior was also subjected to experimentation to create just the right environment.

hedgehog – as a guide. Lotus then applied clay to that depth and back it went to MGA to be copy-milled into the final clay buck. The surface was scanned, and the information was used to generate the full-size clay model in what turned out to be an extremely messy process.

The initial clay model came back to the factory in May 1994, and the design was signed off by the product committee. This body included Adrian Palmer, Roger Becker, Hugh Kemp, Andrew Walmsley, Romano Artioli and Giampaulo Benedini, but, significantly, by 1998 only Roger Becker was still active at Lotus – as head of chassis engineering.

This then gave the design department the approval for the shape of the vehicle, so that it was quite well defined by this point. The designers took plaster moulds from the clay, and these were used to generate the fibreglass bodies for the first prototypes and also to produce the masters for the final sets of production moulds. There were numerous tweaks along the way, where modifications needed to be made to the panels, and it was very much a hands-on process, involving the clay, the plaster and the fibreglass.

MODELLING CIRCUIT

Andy Hill worked on the car for 18 months, during which time he worked both with Julian and the modellers to create the shape of the outside of the car. There were between four and six modellers working on the full-size clay at any given time, depending on the area under discussion. Most of them were Lotus employees, although some contract modellers were hired as and when the design studio's fluctuating workload demanded. Andy said:

> There are some very good people working on the contract modelling circuit, and they could be working for as little as one or two weeks, or perhaps six months or so. When a design comes to fruition, they are laid off, but although it's rather an odd lifestyle, they work and play hard and it's very well paid, and they could be off to work in Germany or somewhere the next week.

Lotus's head modeller is Roger Godfrey, and all this work goes on in the design studio. The modellers generally worked with one person on the front, one on the back, and a couple on the interior, as the design was re-evaluated to encompass thing like headlamp height, wheel coverage, windscreen shape. Because the car is so light, its aerodynamics are particularly important. However, Lotus weren't looking for an especially low drag coefficient because top speed was not the overriding factor, so styling did not have to be sacrificed on the altar of aerodynamic efficiency. It was necessary to achieve a good aerodynamic balance between the front and the back end, between how much lift and how much downforce was desirable. Andy continued:

> Numerous aspects were continually massaged to get the shape to where everyone was in agreement. That meant the production department, the engineering department, the legal people – everyone had to buy into that and sign the bit of paper, which is why it ended up being done in several stages. When the full-size model was approved, we could go forward from there, but it was all against a pretty tight deadline and there were always compromises to be made. The handling and performance stemmed from light weight and engineering factors, so we were always arguing about which bits of the body needed to be changed to meet those targets.

The interior and the exterior were being designed at the same time. Because the radiator duct at the front reduces the amount of lift at the front of the car, the back end became unbalanced, lifting under aerodynamic load, which was undesirable in a rear-drive car. As mentioned elsewhere, this particular imbalance was the subject of an argument between Julian Thomson and Lotus aerodynamicist Richard 'Windy' Hill at the MIRA wind tunnel. The car spent several days at a time there. The areas in question were blocked in very roughly using lumps of clay, Styrofoam and tape to build up the surfaces in order to attain aerodynamic balance. Said Andy Hill:

> A minor internal battle raged between Lotus designers and wind tunnel boffins as aesthetics vied for supremacy over aerodynamics. Conversely, however, an interesting aspect of the Elise is that its body designer and its chassis designer are very good friends, and this undoubtedly had a bearing on the efficiency of the project and the nature of the completed car. In the very early stages of the project the conflict that can exist between the engineering and styling was absent, and Julian Thomson and Richard Rackham established the parameters very quickly.

TRICKS OF THE TRADE

Andy Hill revealed some of the tricks of the trade. The clay model looks flat and dull in its plain terracotta colour. But cover it with foil and it comes alive. The foil enables the designer to see the highlights on the car. The material is called 'dynock', which is a flexible film and it comes either self-coloured or can be sprayed any colour the designer chooses. Masses of plasticizer are put into the paint and it's used when the paint is really green – nearly dry. Then the whole sheet is immersed in a bucket of hot water, after which the backing is peeled off and it can be stretched taut over the surface of the model. The clay can be made to look like a painted surface and, as with the foil, the dynock-covered car shows off the highlights.

> This enables us to make sure the contours are accurate and the surface is even. You don't normally see all these lines on the car. It's a bit like going through a tunnel and you see all the strip lights reflected in a car's paintwork. And these lines enable us to manipulate the shape so that when you see the car in real life in normal light you see these beautiful highlights in the way the lines flow along the car. Like the way the lines form an 'S' over the shape of the wheelarch.
>
> It's quite an art, because you can manipulate the surface only a very small amount and really change radically how the light is reflected off it.

This is one of the reasons why the designers work in clay – because it's so adaptable. They can take more off, or put more on and reapply the dynock film. But basically, this fiddling around with the highlights of what has been agreed as the final shape is making changes that only the designers fully appreciate. 'It's the difference between looking at the car and thinking "that's OK", and thinking, "that's really perfect",' said Andy. 'Getting it right doesn't just happen overnight.'

SUPER SPORTS MOTORCYCLES

When marshalling their thoughts on the Elise project, it was from their Ducatis that stylist Julian Thomson and project engineer Richard Rackham took their cues. During the Elise's gestation period in 1996 the 916 Ducati was the state of the art super sports motorcycle – rivalled only by the mass-produced Honda CBR900 FireBlade – and notwithstanding Ducati's reputation for unreliability, the 916 was nothing less than an icon. Its tried-and-tested V-twin with desmodromic cam-operated valve gear had been around since 1955, and the alloy spaceframe chassis was a delight. The way the exhaust cans exited under the seat was a styling coup, and its fairing panels – inevitably Italian racing red – with projecting twin headlights and elegantly curved screen were unquestionably the sharpest around.

Ducatis are lightweight machines, and well engineered. Ducati have a racing pedigree virtually as long as Lotus's, and their bikes all look fabulous. Ducati prices, too, are notably higher than their rivals' are, including Triumph, who joined the Japanese in the competition for state-of-the-art styling and performance with their T595 Daytona at the end of 1996. Ducatis are made in smaller numbers than Triumph, let alone the Japanese models, so they are by definition more exclusive. All of this makes them rich boys' toys, which coincidentally, is actually the segment at which the Elise is aimed. Thomson and

Rackham almost deliberately translated all these elements into the Elise.

JULIAN THOMSON, PAST AND FUTURE

Outside the factory gate, Rackham and Thomson were friends, and the pair rode out together on their Ducatis. Their rapport extended to each being best man at the other's wedding. Besides his Ducati, Rackham also owns a classic 'gentleman's' motorcycle, a 1952 in-line twin-cylinder Sunbeam S7, featuring then-new and unique componentry including car-type engine and gearbox, shaft-drive, generator, distributor and cast aluminium silencer. He attributes his early interest in engineering to his boyhood Meccano set – something many of us had, but which in my case was more often assembled by my father with me as the hapless observer. Aged eleven, Rackham rebuilt a Cyclemaster moped engine, which he discovered burned out on the Norfolk coast, using Araldite to bond together the ruptured fuel tank. The adhesive medium he employed was a portent of things to come.

The close partnership between Rackham and Thomson was not destined to last at Hethel, however, as in August 1998 Julian moved to Barcelona to head up Volkswagen's design studio. He viewed the prospect with a mixture of enthusiasm and pragmatism: 'It'll be good to work for a mainstream car manufacturer, designing VWs and Audis, and maybe Bentleys as well,' he said. 'And it's the first chance I've had to work abroad, so that'll be fun.'

6 Testing Times

I met up with two of the key figures in the Elise programme in the Lotus Social Club. Alastair McQueen and Dave Minter were taking a break in the first floor of the old Second World War airfield control tower, which must now be many times more comfortable than was ever originally intended.

Designing and refining cars has an element of saloon bar chat about it, as the first thing designers talk about is what they would like to see in their own cars, such as future technologies, race car construction, a composite monocoque perhaps; as it turned out, extrusion was an early suggestion. Extrusions can create a similar sort of structure to what you might find in a F1 car, in terms of lightness and rigidity, and complicity with crash regulations. Clearly these ideas meant moving away from the backbone chassis-type structure that had been Lotus tradition since the first Elan and into lightweight structures. They appreciated the significance of this move not simply for crash-worthiness but in making the cars handle well. As Dave put it:

Lotus is not just a manufacturing company, and the decision was taken to go this route because it would make us the world leaders in this sort of structure. And similarly the same sort thinking went into the brakes, because we are the first people in the world to come up with this production method for the discs, so it's a shop window for what engineering people can do for other clients. There's an awful lot of development, and considering the time frame in which we chose to put ourselves to develop the vehicle, it was quite a risk to take at the time.

Dave Minter is executive engineer, vehicle development. He was a member of the original Elise team and worked closely with Tony Shute on project management and ride and handling. He admits to 'driving a desk' much of the time, but was snapped here before taking the author out for an unforgettable ride in the Elise Sport.

While the Elise's conception and evolution was a team effort, Dave Minter was responsible for co-ordinating all the developmental aspects of the car, ensuring that the brakes complemented the handling and the steering. His wealth of experience meant that he was also involved to an extent in the design process helping to prevent problems occurring with the Elise that had occurred with the Elan and Esprit. He said:

> The Elan was a different vehicle altogether. The main criticism levelled at the Elan was that it had no significant driver input. It virtually drove itself. Somebody with limited ability could still drive it quickly, but there was none of the adjustability that a switched-on driver could get out of the Elise. Ultimately the Elise is probably slower, especially in the wet, because it hasn't got the stability of the Elan. But it has got the ability for the driver to make it do things that the Elan can't offer. It's a lot to do with front-wheel drive versus rear-wheel drive. The Elan has all the characteristics of a Lotus – the linear controls and tactile qualities that all our cars have – but the fundamental difference is that it's extremely easy to drive but doesn't involve the driver like the Elise does. That's where the big pleasure comes in. You really have to feel what the Elise is doing, get it on the edge and feel for a little bit more here, a little bit more there! It's a big smile! Anyone can drive a GTi quickly, but this is a different sort of car. We looked at it in a different way, at the Elan's good qualities and at some of the bad press it had got, and we tried to major on the positive things and apply them to the Elise. I had a fundamental belief in the Elise, and I hope that all the things that I wanted to put into the car have helped to make it the success that it is.

> The intimate part of the testing is to get all the pedal feels the same; the linearity of the vehicle's responses – whether it's brakes, throttle or steering – has to be very progressive, so that when you're driving on a knife edge your brain can understand exactly what's happening to the car. If you have a non-linear car, say one that's got servo brakes, you'll apply too much brake too early and you'll end up taking your foot off. If you have a linear car, once you've braked once you'll immediately know how much you've got to put on in future, because it's a linear thing. It's the same with steering. If you don't have this feedback you won't have confidence in the car. Driving it should be an enjoyable experience: as we say, if it ain't fun, it ain't a Lotus. And fun is not being scared of a car; fun is enjoying the car. Some manufacturers believe that if your car is fighting you all the way, that is the ultimate macho machine. We've driven cars around here that you're fighting all the time, and we don't subscribe to that at all.

DAVE MINTER: CO-ORDINATOR

First and foremost it was necessary to set out a task list that would make the Elise the car that they wanted it to be. Dave Minter explained the development program from first prototype stage, and spoke passionately about the car's virtues on the road.

> Driving the first prototype tells you where you are on the scale of things. The first one we drove was the day we had broken up for Christmas 1994. There was no body on it – it was just a rolling chassis. Richard Rackham and Tony Shute did a lap round

the circuit about half past ten at night, and that gave us so much confidence that it was going to be right.

We've driven different Lotus products and different types of cars around here and very often something will start shaking. We knew immediately that we were on to a winner here because it had this torsional rigidity as well as a certain minimalism because of the light weight. As soon as you touched the steering it was there; it was doing what you wanted to do and, quite honestly, it was a revelation. Here was a car that you could take by the scruff of the neck and you could drive as you wished. Everybody was fired with enormous enthusiasm.

The staff were working overtime, having set themselves a target to get the car running on the track, but there was a long way to go before the final specification was settled. A great many changes to the damper settings, for example.

'You can spend 20 per cent of your time getting 80 per cent there, so it's the last few changes that are critical, and they take a lot more time to achieve. It is also knowing you have gone as far as you can go, as well,' said Dave.

Lotus actually produced twelve prototypes. The early ones were used for legislative crash tests, and when Lotus were sure that they complied, the later cars were used for tuning evaluation purposes. There was also a process of continuous development, and the engineers are still looking at areas where they might wrest a little bit more out of it.

Tyre development is also crucial. There have been huge strides in tyre technology in the past twenty years and it is amazing what difference the right set of tyres can make to a car's behaviour. Lotus had the opportunity to do some development work with the supplier – in this case Pirelli – to optimize the tyres to their requirements. They tried lots of tyres of various sorts in the sizes that we have for the car, and Pirellis were deemed to be the most suitable for the Elise, a blend of performance and price. Another aspect Lotus are mindful of is all-round, all-weather performance. A small amount of grip is sacrificed in order to elevate the wet grip performance of the car, so the driver is not caught out by any of its characteristics.

Lotus were initially very concerned – before they developed the car – that it wasn't going to have enough top speed, and they accordingly carried out some performance tests. Although clearly the most important aspects of vehicle performance are acceleration, braking and handling, and these are ultimately more important than straight-line speed. In-gear acceleration is more important than 0–60mph (0–100km/h) acceleration. As we know, 50–70mph (80–112km/h) and 30–50mph (48–80km/h) in the gears are much more relevant to real life driving. The Elise is a two-seater sports car powered by the same engine as the MGF, but the lightness and the character of the Elise make it completely different to the MG.

'One of the original aims was to create a sub-6 seconds 0–60mph car,' said Dave. 'Initial predictions were something like 5.9 seconds, and on the Millbrook straight it clocked 5.7, which was quite a historic moment because we got something better than we expected.'

PRIORITIES RIGHT

Lotus wanted to put the money into the technology and character of the new car rather than tool up specially for ancillary components. Part of Dave's job is to find parts from other vehicles that will do for Lotus models, like door locks or mirrors. He explained:

> It's no good putting all the money into wonderful door handles if you haven't developed the dampers. I remember in the early days when we started the project I was trying to find a door lock. It couldn't cost a lot of money, because we couldn't afford to tool up something like that ourselves, and one of the crucial aspects of this car is that we had a very limited amount of money. We decided we wanted to put that money into new technology, we wanted to put the limited resources we had into specific items that were to do with enhancement of the vehicle.
>
> Take the door mirror. It comes from a Metro, but if we were to tool up to make our own door mirror, it would cost maybe as much as what the entire vehicle cost. It's absolutely astronomical what it costs to make things like that. So what I have to do is locate one that looks right with the car, but also has to serve a legal function. The field of view has to be acceptable. But different markets call for different glasses, so we have to identify a manufacturer who

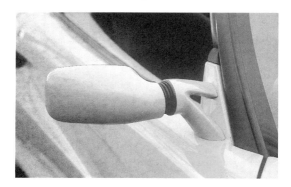

The door mirror was sourced from the Metro parts bin to minimize development costs: if Lotus made their own it could cost as much as the entire vehicle.

makes the right shape mirror plus interchangeable glasses. That's one development task!

Another example is the windscreen wiper. The design brief was for a single item, and the Elise windscreen wiper works fantastically well. It's probably the best wiper system Lotus have had, and it's an in-house design. However, a major wiper manufacturer wanted a cool £100,000 before they would even attempt to design and productionize what Lotus wanted, and that immediately cut them out of the scheme. 'Richard [Rackham] designed something that worked, which was made up in the workshop, and eventually a small company was found who produced the necessary parts for it. But it was all very time consuming,' said Dave.

The Elise wiper is an extremely good design aerodynamically. As the radiator sucks air up the front and over the bonnet, it flows up in a pattern, so it is always in line with the wiper; as a result you don't get any cross wind and you don't get any lift when you travel at high speed. It is always difficult with a steep curvature to ensure that the glass is wiped over a sufficient area, but Lotus has managed to do it.

I asked whether the soft top was as aerodynamically sound as a closed coupé, and it is, so long as the roof is in place. This is partly due to the screen design; it's no coincidence that the Elan was virtually the same, with a similarly shaped windscreen. It directs the airflow over the top of the car, and it's feasible to cruise at motorway speeds with the top off. But of course there is a hard top if you want, or if the climate demands it. The materials that are used in the cockpit are virtually all weatherproof so that nothing is going to get damaged if it get wets in a shower.

SLIPPED DISCS

Dave went on to talk about the Elise's brakes.

> I'm particularly pleased with the brakes, because they help you feel very comfortable with the car. You feel you are in control of the brake all the time and you can go round the circuit at ten-tenths all day and you never run out of brakes. It's also a car you can take to the circuit quite easily; if you can't get your fun on the road then it's quite capable of going on the circuit without any modifications whatsoever.

True enough. This was one of the first concepts to be agreed – the Seven heritage coming to the fore – so the suspension and chassis were designed with a view to the car being used in competition at some stage. Its ride height and the geometry were changed substantially to accommodate what became the competition version, the 190, which also has the composite clamshells.

The new metal matrix disc brakes were very much an unknown quantity, although Lotus were aware that several manufacturers were testing similar metal matrix set-ups. Initially Lotus didn't know how they would perform in adverse conditions, so they did a substantial amount of testing at Millbrook.

> It's good there because you circulate round the banking. Here [Hethel], where if you have a brake failure you are very much in the soup. But if you have a brake failure at Millbrook you coast round until you come to a halt. As it turned out, we just could not believe how easily the car stopped. We also had to make sure that the pedal effort was acceptable because there was no servo. It soon became clear that because there was no weight in the car the pedal effort was entirely acceptable.

Without a servo it is easy to brake late because you know how much pressure to apply to the pedal. On the other hand, if you are involved in an emergency situation and you have ABS it's very easy to apply too much pressure and lock up the wheels. You then have to take your foot off some way and then reapply the pressure, and that's not an easy thing to do in an emergency. Find yourself in that situation with the Elise and its hard pedal, you only have to lift your foot a millimetre and the wheels spin again.

> We spent much of our time discovering and harnessing that capability. Most manufacturers' goal is 1G – they're satisfied with that figure. The Elise brakes at 1.2G, because we wanted to provide control by enabling the driver to feather the brake, increasing pedal pressure and lifting off. ABS has to be an average, taking into account weather conditions, different road conditions and surfaces, so it's an average algorithm. The Elise talks to you. You can feel what it's doing, you can feel the tyres squirm as it starts to lock up. In any situation you'll brake much quicker than with ABS. We didn't actually find that out until we started to experiment and really push the car.

By late 1998 it was clear that there were problems productionizing the metal matrix discs, but it was anticipated that Brembo would be able to make them in sufficient quantity to satisfy the SE models, which would give it an added value distinction. Lanxide never managed to create the disc as a moulded part, and the MMC disc was only made as a relatively crude sand casting. All the cars made up to the time that Lanxide went bust in mid-1998 had the MMC discs, but Lotus quickly pressed traditional cast iron discs into service.

> We're back with known technology with cast iron discs. We have to prove Brembo's ability to make the MMC discs in a production tool, which is what Lanxide failed to do. Sand casting is not only a crude method but it's expensive. Richard and I packaged the biggest disc we could in the first place, because no one knew how the MMC discs would perform. It turns out that the Elise is over-braked now, and we're happy that we can move up to the 145bhp SE spec knowing the car will stop all right.

During the development process the engineers spent some time in Norfolk and then took the prototypes off on longer runs to other parts of the country as well as abroad to see how they behaved on a typical French autoroute:

> That's to say, smooth but with a lot of primary ride influence, long waves in groups. And then in Germany, where you can run at fairly high speeds for longer periods on constant radius corners. A mix of driving environments is very important for vehicle development.
>
> We had developed our own tests that we could do here in Norfolk, a number of precision stops that we could feel comfortable with and check for mechanical failure. We did the first test at Millbrook, we did a lot of work around Hethel on brake fade, and we wanted to find out what the 'fadeability' of the installation was like. We didn't know what the brakes would do. If you have a big disc and heat it up, it will move in a manner that's called 'coning'. It'll push the pistons out, so when

it goes straight again you're left with a gap between the disc and the pad, which you have to take up with pedal travel. We found that the MMC discs weren't at all prone to coning.

Even so, the Elise is the first car in the world to run with MMC brake discs, so Lotus had to be absolutely certain there were not going to be any mistakes. They did a lot of work on the test track because they recognized that the threshold temperature of the metal matrix disc is 450°C, at which point the surface starts to melt into little globules, which impregnate the pads. The testers needed to find out how many stops the discs would tolerate before meltdown occurred. They couldn't achieve any more than 200°C, so they developed an acceleration and deceleration test from 30 to 80mph and back again to put more heat into the brakes.

Even after eight such tests the discs failed to overheat, so the next step was to take the car to the Stelvio Pass in the Italian Alps, which encompasses most of the worst driving conditions you're likely to experience. It's become recognized as a motor industry standard, along with the Grossglockner Pass, which isn't so severe.

Dave and Alastair agree that there is no sterner trial in a real life situation. They placed themselves in the position of an enthusiastic owner, and drove as quickly as possible down the winding Stelvio Pass, with its multitude of hairpin bends, to evaluate the brakes and to make sure the car was quite comfortable doing it. Dave recalled:

> Driving the Stelvio is different from just driving a test track quickly, because the conditions vary. You can do lots of laps of specific tracks but they won't necessarily yield all the information you need,

whereas the Stelvio, which is very severe, with lots of hairpins, enables us to assess the cooling period between corners. Of course, the faster you go the less cooling time there is between applications, and the more pressure you put on the brakes. Also, some of our customers might drive it, so we needed to make sure the car works there before they do. We just put ourselves in the position of the customer – they go there and they thrash down the road as fast as they can. It's a real hoot!

Obviously the temperature of aluminium metal matrix brake discs is different to cast iron. The critical temperature is 450°C, when the surface layer starts to melt. With cast iron discs it's 700°C. But an aluminium disc will lose the heat faster, so there's a gain in that respect. Although it has a lower optimum maximum temperature, the ability to dissipate heat is much higher than with cast iron.

This statistic was established after one of these tests, the car having rushed down the hill in fourth gear, braking as hard as possible, accelerating repeatedly out of every corner. Dave outlined the method.

At the bottom you turn off the road and come to a halt; you put your foot on the brake and measure the pedal pressure. Then you wait for ten minutes and measure it again. With conventional cast iron discs you'd be running at 600–650°C, and that heat would have dissipated all over the car and found its way into the fluid. But we are running at virtually half that temperature, and there is no difference in pedal travel after ten minutes. So the by-product of all this is you don't lose your brakes, or get aeration in them, nor does the fluid boil, because it just never gets to that sort of temperature.

Dave described a formative experience with the car when they were doing some of the original tyre evaluation.

I can remember the first time I drove the car on the road. I was the first person to do so. It was the car's road-going debut, and we drove it to MIRA to do some tyre work in the wet; I had to keep waiting for the tyre company guy to catch me up. I was determined to go the cross-country route that we regularly use, and I thought that it would bring out the qualities of the car if they were there. This was all along back roads, and I just enjoyed it so much. When I got there I told everybody this car is so exciting to drive. I hated waiting for the guy to catch me up.

The Elise was taken to a couple of other circuits during its durability cycle. The first was Nardo, an 8-mile (13km) circuit owned by Fiat near Lecce in southern Italy. It is used by the industry for durability and high temperature work. Ambient temperatures of 44°C are not uncommon there, and the car may be driven flat out and parked up in full sun to assess how well the cooling system and thermostat are working. The engineers had to make sure that the cooling fan worked, that the radiator was the right size, and that the pipework was adequate and the engine didn't boil over even when the radiator was partially covered with bugs. They needed to make sure the air ducting that had been proven in the wind tunnel actually worked in practice. At Nardo Lotus were also able to scrutinize further the brakes and the aerodynamics, as the car needed to feel good at full speed. Conversely, they also ran a 'Lecce city cycle', driving around the town logging speeds and temperatures in a comparatively hot environment. Dave commented:

We've done three trips to Nardo. We learn a lot by driving it down there. The first time I went there was in 1979 and we drove there non-stop, in an Esprit and an Eclat! It was 1,760 miles [2,830km], and took a little over 24 hours. That was the sort of thing we used to do in those days. Mike Kimberley and Tony Rudd once drove an Elan to Rome and back in a weekend and they thought that was a good benchmark, and people used to volunteer to drive test cars down there.

On the way back from Nardo the route home up the Adriatic coast took the Elise to the Stelvio pass, and the first year the testers went on to the Nürburgring circuit near Cologne. So many myths and legends have grown up around this highly demanding 14-mile (22km) circuit that it was felt that the Elise should also be tried there.

We could only get the brake temperatures up to 120 there, braking for the Adenau bridge, which is nothing. Tony took it for

two or three laps but then it started pouring with rain so we thought discretion was the better part of valour! You must try it – we did a lot of testing for a tyre company there, but it's a public road and you can drive it for about DM4. The best drivers in the long-distance races there are the BMW and Porsche factory test drivers, who routinely drive it day after day. That was why we wanted to try the Elise there, just to see where we were with it. Now, you can take a standard Elise and drive it all day at ten-tenths around any circuit and you won't lose your brakes.

With the car up and running, selling better than ever, and gaining plaudits from the press, Lotus have naturally concentrated durability work to make sure it stays that way.

We treat durability work as two sections. One is carried out here, where cars are driven around the track by different drivers, who log all the data and see how they go. They are hard miles too. The

The Elise is equally at home on the road or on a race circuit, and its development programme took in the test tracks at MIRA, Nardo and the old Nürburgring. Here Tony Shute powers the Elise Sport out of a hairpin on the Prescott hillclimb.

154

80,000-mile [130,000km] test car has just been to Zolder, and it's got our engine performance kit on too, which is a way of evaluating that. During the development stage, we also ran three 30,000-mile [48,000km] durability cars at Millbrook to give us confidence that they were sound. There's a durability cycle at Millbrook, which means that you go on the gravel road to get gravel ingress into the car; you do two or three laps of the high-speed circuit; you do the hill route, which means going through the gears, stopping on gradients and backing up. And you go through this set procedure for 30,000 miles, logging what happens to the car, what falls off and what breaks. Each car did 30,000 miles. We ran an early car, which we learned a lot from, a car in the middle of the development programme, and one of the pre-production cars also ran on that cycle. We also did salt corrosion tests at Millbrook to see how the aluminium chassis and steel parts would stand up to salt corrosion. And that was all before the car went on sale.

The 30,000-mile test is a way of compressing a host of different conditions into a concentrated period. The work was contracted out to Millbrook, which is a General Motors subsidiary and employs its own test drivers. Each of the Elise 30,000-mile tests were carried out over a six-month period. Lotus carried out similar tests with the Esprit and the Elan, so they had datum points from those models to compare with and relate to the Elise. Before any of these tests could be carried out they had to subject a prototype (vehicle number four) to the rigours of Millbrook's notorious Belgian pavé section to make sure the chassis didn't come apart. It travelled a gruelling 1,000 miles (1,600km) at 30mph (48km/h), which resulted in the

rear subframe being replaced with a steel version.

That's what makes us different from our competitors. People like Caterham and TVR don't do that sort of testing, although the Seven has been around for so long they know every last nut and bolt. But when you produce a new car with a new chassis and different brakes, you have to be confident of it before you put it onto the market-place. Any problems we had were engineered out.

TYPE APPROVAL

Lotus made one of the early prototypes available for type approval tests, and Ken Sears went over to Holland to the Dutch facility, where more than 50 per cent of the tests were carried out in a series of three visits. Although type approval for the car was obtained in the Netherlands, the tests were not fundamentally different from what they would have been in the UK. Dave said:

They're very keen over there, and they gave us a few pointers on what we'd need to change in order to get full certification. We had to work on things like radii on particular parts of the body – where there had to be a minimum 3mm radius perhaps. We had to fiddle around with things like that. But normally a manufacturer sends off a finished car to homologation, and they might find there's a serious problem with one of the radii. That puts a project back six months. Lotus, on the other hand, had tested every possible driving circumstance, so that they had all the relevant data before they came to the homologation tests and we knew the car would pass.

The main hurdle was the crash test, and the engine was emissions certified for European spec. One of the great cost savings of this programme was that we used an engine and gearbox that was already certified for Europe, and we didn't have to do anything more. Originally we thought we might have to recalibrate the ECU, but once we'd driven the car we found it was quite adequate. To this day we've never had a K-series motor on the test bed. The authorities were quite happy to accept our findings with the car up and running with that engine. It saved us a fortune.

To obtain type approval they had to crash two or three cars into a barrier at 30mph to satisfy frontal impact requirements, which were passed very easily. There were also emissions regulations to be complied with.

The only other foreign markets we do are Japan and Australia; we didn't want to venture elsewhere because we couldn't justify the amount of engineering work required to be compliant with other countries. At the moment we have got a waiting list of two years on all the cars we can possibly manufacture in this factory.

By autumn 1998 Lotus had a test car coming up for 80,000 miles. A performance test showed it to be 0.1 seconds faster now than it was three months earlier. Although Lotus use the Hethel track purely for off-limit handling and running top-secret and prototype cars, they drive cars outside the plant as soon as they can, and much experience is gained driving on the road in real life situations.

'The final niceties of the car really come from our experiences of driving on the road,' said Dave. I can only agree, as I certainly enjoyed taking the Elise on the open road – where you're confronted with an infinite variety of surfaces, gradients, cambers and traffic situations – far more pleasurable and informative than hammering around the test track.

Dave commented that Lotus have come across vehicles from other manufacturers that have been developed on a proving ground, and it's as if they have never seen any real-world road situations. So they regard the track as an opportunity to study the car's behaviour under extreme conditions, and carry out a lot of test work that would be strictly illegal on the road.

However, there's a good mix of road types close to home in Norfolk, which present a variety of conditions for evaluating changes to suspension settings. Dave highlighted the new Wymondham bypass, which is a seamless concrete construction but which has a high tyre polish-generating surface. He likes to go to round some of the back lanes to the south of Norwich, which are among the most uneven in the country, and from the handling point of view are absolutely ideal. However, as Dave agreed, it's getting more and more difficult to drive fast on the roads in the UK, where the traditional supercar is more or less redundant, so your only other option is to get your kicks on a race circuit.

That's where the Elise is particularly good. You don't need to change anything, you don't even have to change the tyre pressures, and you'll have a damn good time. Having said that, you can have fun at 50mph [80km/h] – it's that sort of car. I believe this is the sports car for the next generation, as it's much more environmentally friendly.

THE SPORT ELISE

You hear it coming and it growls at you, and it has that low-slung demeanour that

Dave Minter prepares to take the factory's Elise Sport demonstrator out onto the test track to provide the author with one of life's formative experiences.

most circuit racers have, that 'don't mess with me' sort of attitude. The yellow Sport Elise, otherwise known as the 190 Motorsport car, is Lotus's competition demonstrator and public relations car, and it's a showcase of the aftermarket accessories that Lotus offers, including the purposeful black Techno Magnesio wheels (6J front, 8J rear), shod with special Yokohama tyres for road and track. It's a very soft tyre, yielding perhaps only 3,000 miles (4,800km) before it wears out, but then it is essentially a track tyre. The Sport Elise has also got cross-drilled cast-iron discs, an uprated anti-roll bar, aftermarket springs and dampers – and it's lowered by 30mm front and rear, which is considerably lower than normal. The Elise has very little overhang, so generally there's no problem with ground clearance. Inside is a hefty roll cage linked to the standard roll-hoop, while door panels and the instrument binnacle are in Kevlar. The seat belts are bolted to the roll-hoop, an RAC-approved installation.

The Sport Elise is powered by the K-series engine, with extensive modifications carried out by Rover, originally for the Rover 200 one-make championship that was canned when BMW took over. These alterations include changes to the head and the crank, rods, pistons and valves and the engine management system. The Elise can do 0–100mph in 10.5 seconds, and 0–60mph in 4.4 seconds. Rover supply the engine to Lotus and Caterham now, and in late 1998 Lotus had sold around forty units of the motorsport car. They compete with success against Vipers and 911s in Germany, Italy, Australia and the USA. Dave said:

It's a shame we can't produce it as a road car. But Rover didn't want us to do that, and we're very much bound to abide by that. As it's a racing engine, they've done no road-going durability validation on it and product liability issues were uppermost in their minds. But we've got the 135bhp kit for the road-going cars and the up-spec SE model. All this kit on the 190 makes you want to go even faster. But people want more. For instance Mark Waldron has a 1.4 turbocharged version that he's hillclimbing with – he's an instructor at Prescott. It's caught people's imagination, and I think Colin Chapman would have liked it. There's so much of

The interior of the Elise Sport is specially equipped with racing seats, full Sparco racing harnesses and a fire extinguisher. Even with belts on, the author was grateful for the support provided by the diagonal brace of the roll cage when hurtled around the Hethel test track by ace development engineer Dave Minter.

that David and Goliath about it, the little car beating the big ones. It's so typical of Chapman, high performance from low mass, plus new technology.

Lotus are involved with the gentlemanly 96 Club, which holds meetings at race circuits including Silverstone, Brands Hatch and Mallory Park; Lotus take the Sport Elise car to these meetings to demonstrate its prowess among a wide variety of machinery, including the odd ex-F1 car.

'On a nice smooth circuit like Silverstone you can run much harder suspension settings,' said Dave. This was a prelude to a demonstration on the somewhat harsher Hethel circuit. Dave indicated the full harness in the passenger seat that I was to install myself in, and once secured, we set off.

'It's got ultra close-ratio straight-cut Quaife internals in a normal PT1 box,' he shouted. 'The regular Sport Elise 190s have a normal close-ratio box.' The volume of noise from the quicker engine was substantially greater. Then we got going in earnest, and the thrust was impressive. As we braked for the chicane on the main straight and the hairpin at the end my body was forced so hard into the crutch straps that I was thankful of my paternity. To offset the discomfort of such violent deceleration I grasped the cross-brace of the roll-over cage and held on tight in the corners. The car's progress here was truly spectacular, clipping apexes and with just a hint of tyre squeal in the tighter turns, and lap after lap we seemed to go faster and faster, gear changes flowing slickly before and after the corners. Here was a man totally in his element, at one with the car, and as we finally rolled to a halt it occurred to me that the experience had been one of those rare life-defining milestones.

Upgrades

Two years down the line, Lotus is reaping the benefits of the Elise. They've responded swiftly to a significant demand from Elise customers for aftermarket parts, such as the shock absorbers and engine upgrades, and it is possible to mix and match suspension kit, roll cage and competition seat belt. But you can also buy a car which has that equipment to start with. It seems to be a car that people want to compete in, one they wish to modify and personalize. This is perhaps surprising when you consider how individualistic the Elise design is, but perhaps it simply reflects a general trend towards niche market vehicles.

Said Dave: 'There's a lot of spin-off from the Elise that we haven't had from other

Lotus's fleet of press vehicles is overseen by Alistair McQueen, whose title is executive engineer, product development. In his role as the firm's chief test track driver he demonstrated just what the Elise is capable of around the Hethel proving ground.

models. We've always tended to produce the basic model with very few variants, but now we produce all these other bits and pieces on the car to deliver it.'

Indeed, there are also other groups who are interested, and Lotus have provided vehicles for a race series in Italy as well as cars for Australia and the USA, while Silverstone Racing School has twelve. It appeared that Silverstone's bookings had shot up because of the Elise course cars, and of course that's also a good sales pitch for Lotus because the pupil may go off and

buy a car. It's in a different league to the average GTi-type car.

ALASTAIR MCQUEEN: CHIEF TEST DRIVER

Alastair McQueen's view of the car is very much how a customer or journalist might perceive it. He does a lot of promotional driving and driver training, as well as looking after the press cars and

Alastair McQueen looks for an apex on a right-hander at the Hethel test track.

The arms cross as opposite lock is applied, and tyres screech while the Elise broadsides its way around the bend.

159

demonstrators. Like Dave Minter, he's a long term Lotus employee, having joined in 1966.

Apart from a short break in the early 80s, I have sort of grown up with company and with several of the cars. I've always been involved with the development of them and it was nice to be able to come in very much at the early design stage of the Elise and apply some influence there as well.

When you're developing the car, you always imagine that you are the customer and that you have just driven 300 miles and you are nearing your home. You really enjoyed the drive, and instead of turning into the drive, you actually go round the block again because you have enjoyed yourself so much, even though your tea is burnt. That has got to be the aiming point. I mean, you wouldn't do it with an MGF. In any case, that appeals to a different niche, and Rover recognized that when they sold us the engine. If they thought there was ever going to be any conflict I don't think they would have sold us the engine.

He stressed that the people who developed the Elise were all-rounders, as well as being involved with everything to do with the chassis.

Alastair spends his working life in Lotuses. He looks after the fleet of demonstrators and press cars, which of course includes Esprits as well as Elises. He provided my introduction to the driving experience on the test track.

'There is a bit of a knack to getting into them,' he said. 'It's an acquired technique, but once you've done it a few times it's simple enough.' He talked to the security people on his mobile to let them know he was out on the track with 'a journalist' – a safety precaution. He took me through a few fairly gentle laps and demonstrated some aspects of the car's handling, describing his actions as we went along. The big roundabout at the end of the circuit is where the fun starts.

The lightness of the car meant that we didn't need any servo systems on the brakes or the steering, and you don't find that purity in everyday cars, where they are all assisted – and in most cases over assisted.

Of course, the driver is always potentially fallible, and ABS is a bonus in

Caning a sports car round a test track and getting paid for it can't be a bad way of earning a living. Alastair McQueen corners the Elise at full chat.

It's virtually impossible to lose an Elise in the dry, but eventually the tortured tyres will cry enough, and it's then that the scenery beckons.

those situations. But if you are doing a test slide, one of the beauties of the Elise is that if you do lock up you can take your foot off the pedal maybe half a mill and the wheels will start turning – you just take it off and reapply. When you are really on the limit, getting the very last inch out of the brake, you can hear the tyres churning, getting to their maximum, and you know that you are going to get out. There is no remoteness or isolation.

He was right. After a few laps of the Hethel test track in an Elise in the company of Alastair McQueen, I found that when you started to lose it, you lifted the brake just one millimetre, and it was very easy to regain control. You start to slide and immediately you can get it back again. Alastair pointed out that you have to actually go past the optimum, because you never know what that optimum is until you have exceeded it.

> Part of our philosophy is that the driver should never be surprised by anything and should always be given plenty of warning of what is imminent in terms of its dynamic behaviour. It is a very intimate experience, in that you bond with the car. We believe that the enjoyment of driving it is being able to feel what is happening to the car: you can feel the steering, what's happening to the chassis, so you have this involvement with the vehicle. It's bit like putting on a glove.
>
> We set up all our cars basically the same way so they are fairly neutral. And if we go round this roundabout and I lift off the throttle, the car goes into oversteer [you have to imagine a soundtrack of shrieking tyres and noise of skidding]. And that's a condition that we build in, so the attitude of the car is adjustable with the throttle in cornering. So cornering is not just about steering input, it is about throttle control as well. We could make a car that was very safe and very stable, which would understeer everywhere, but you can make the Elise understeer as well [more tortured tyre noises], so you have the ability to control the car with steering input and throttle control. And that's why it's so much fun.

As we went ever faster round the roundabout, I sensed the demon lurking inside this placid Scot. He was obviously enjoying himself to the full, and providing lurid sideways action for cameraman Tom Wood to snap. It was only a matter of time before we joined the scenery. He remarked:

> The tyres give up first. They get so hot that they just cry enough! There's a degree of lift-off oversteer; when you come off the throttle the car wants to slide off from the rear ultimately, but that is what the fineness of balance is all about. The communication you get through the steering is very precise. It gives you a lot of information, but without any kickback through the steering, so if you're in a bumpy corner and the wheels lock, you can pull through it without any unnecessary wrestling with the wheel.

Sure enough, it swapped ends, but Alastair kept it on the road. Then it was my turn.

7   Driving the Elise

Without doubt, the Elise is the most exhilarating car I've driven. There! I've said it, and that's some admission, considering things like 911s, TVRs, Caterhams and assorted Lotuses that I've crossed swords with in the past. My racing Alfa GTV6 was fun, but was as unwieldy as the Elise is nimble. These days, everything on even faintly sporting family cars is over-assisted, to my mind, making the driver remote from the road and the sensations of driving. My current tin-top Alfa 155 V6 may turn in well and be a bit faster in a straight line, but who cares when the Elise can be tossed around with such abandon?

If much of the Elise's inspiration came from motorcycles, it satisfies in one area that two wheels can't, which is that, for short runs at least, I could strap my two young children together in the passenger

The Elise steering is very direct and can be controlled with the fingertips – the smallest input makes for a change of direction. Although he thought the seats somewhat lacking in padding, John Tipler found the driving position perfectly adequate, with hands at ten to two and legs virtually straight ahead.

seat and squeeze the dog in the footwell and hang the squabbling. In the 'money no object' stakes, I'd have one like a shot. I may well be preaching to the converted here, but in any case let me assure you that you'd never get tired of driving it, and neither would you ever get bored of looking at it.

Before getting on with my eulogy, I'll deliver the downside first. If there is one shortcoming about the Elise driving experience, it's actually the driver's seat. It's just too spartan. There's not enough padding underneath your backside, and it doesn't afford grip when you need it in corners. I had a plain Sparco racing seat in my Alfa that was adequate, but I could still move around in it when cornering, which was disconcerting. So like many other people, I customized it by filling a couple of bin-liners with a two-pack chemical – like a cavity wall insulator – placed them in the seat and promptly sat in it. The stuff set almost instantly, and my posterior shape was enshrined in foam. No way could I move around when cornering after that. You could do the same in the Elise bucket seats, or simply have Lotus install a more upmarket seat.

What they do provide is a little black squeezy pump like the doctor takes your blood pressure with, down beside your left hip, with which you can inflate the backrest to provide more or less lumbar support. My daughter Zoë suggested it could be for inflating the tyres, but in fact it proved to be a welcome facility on a long run, where the seat-back pressure could be

The ignition keys dangle from the ignition switch and rest on the driver's right knee, which can be irritating, and the ignition lock can prove troublesome.

increased or deflated while travelling along, and you could thus achieve a reasonable compromise. I came to the conclusion that the seat still lacked under-thigh support, though, and if it were mine I'd have to get a seat with a longer squab and with a bit more meat in it. I don't recall ever having had a car that induced the driving position that I found myself adopting most often. It reminded me of Dustin Hoffman in the Alfa Romeo Duetto in *The Graduate*, in which he's sitting round-backed and round-shouldered up against the wheel. Nothing wrong with that; it just seemed different.

Gripe number two, which I noticed instantly at Hethel, even before I was lent the first press car, was that the keys dangle from the ignition switch and rest on or inside your right knee (assuming it's a right-hand drive car), and the irritation of this never completely disappeared. Furthermore, on the first car I borrowed (orange), the ignition lock was sometimes not happy about turning on, and on occasions I spent minutes trying to persuade it to work; however, the yellow car I borrowed subsequently was no problem at all.

The amazing thing about the Elise steering is how direct it is. It's fingertip light, so only the smallest input is needed for a change of direction. It's so agile that any apex can be clipped with spot-on precision. The way you address the steering wheel is with elbows bent and

163

hands at ten to two, and for this six-footer, there's a reasonably straight-legged seating position pushing you back into the seat. Your right knee nestles comfortably against the side of the chassis. The driver's seat is biased towards the centreline of the car, and the passenger seat is immovably fixed further back.

As you'd expect of a car built by the past masters of thrilling sports cars, throttle response was instantaneous, and the car would rip away from traffic light situations in second and third gear. The orange car's gearshift felt a bit rubbery, and although it wasn't unpleasant, it lacked the more desirable metallic, 'notchy' feel. This may have been due to the linkage being some distance to the rear, and although there was no problem engaging the forward gears, it wasn't too happy about going into reverse. On the yellow car, which was virtually brand new – just 1,500 miles (2,400km) on the clock – all systems were absolutely perfect, with not a hint of reluctance or rubbery feel about the gearshift or transmission to engage.

The 1.8-litre K-series performance can be described as athletic at low speed, absolutely scintillating on bendy country roads, and more than adequate on fast A-roads. It's a gutsy engine, and quite adequate for the car in standard trim, although a rasping exhaust note might have made it sound more convincing. The Elise will idle along at just under 1,000rpm if you so wish, and as you pootle along at low revs it feels like, well, any small car, if you discount the austere cockpit. But as you increase speed it shrugs its shoulders and really does want to get cracking, all the way up to 100mph (160km/h).

The Elise isn't a motorway car, though, and at no time did it feel especially powerful, when perhaps its lines suggest that it might be. Only in first and second is

there any hint of a kick in the back as the car surges forward. This is something of a contrast with a traditional 1,700cc Ford-engined Caterham Super Sprint, which certainly behaves like an animal in every gear, even if its out-and-out performance is no greater than the Elise's. However, my outing with Dave Minter in the Elise Sport Motorsport model was another matter, serving to whet the appetite for the few more horses that the 111S version would provide.

The ride is taut yet far from uncomfortable, but almost predictably the rear end does respond with a bang if you go over a pothole or similar abrupt depression. The suspension is pretty noisy on the undulating back roads that characterize much of rural Norfolk, but there's not a hint of the scuttle shake that bedevils many modern wannabe sports cars. And although it may be a bit of a bone-shaking ride on some surfaces, one was left with the impression that it would go a lot quicker if required.

Once or twice it pulled to the right under braking, which I presumed to be a consequence of sticking callipers. But by and large the MMC brakes were fiercely efficient and confidence-inspiring. You knew they were going to anchor up in safety at known hazards, and that encouraged you to approach them going much faster than normal.

I found myself wondering just how long it's going to be possible to enjoy a car like this. It's so far removed from the mundane mediocrity of most cars that the contrast is even more acute when the inevitable traffic jams bring playtime to a halt. Maybe you simply derive your pleasure from those few bursts of driving pleasure that the Elise gives you access to and just put up with the bottlenecks. One could take to the racetrack with an Elise Sport 190, but with

Roundabouts are a great source of entertainment in an Elise and the author found one in particular that he circumnavigated a number of times just for the hell of it.

such a car gridlocks come very expensive. That's pretty negative, I know, but it was the car's very competence that made me think of it.

When I was first shown the ropes on the Hethel test track by press car supremo Alastair McQueen, he put the car through its paces so I could see just what its limits were. The circuit is composed of some of the old wartime runways and perimeter roads, and is in less than tip-top condition in some places. Nevertheless it is an awe-inspiring thought that some of the all-time greats such as Clark, Rindt and Peterson tested F1 Lotuses around there. At one end of the circuit is a loop, not much bigger than an average roundabout, and Alastair attacked it, taking the Elise ever faster and going from lock-to-lock, booting and feathering the throttle to keep the car on the black stuff. Only when the Pirellis were really hot and bothered did the car cry enough and perform a swift pirouette.

When you have access to a fun car for a limited period, you make as much use of it as possible, and so it was with the Lotus. During my week's tenure of the orange car, there was never any question of it running out of grip, although natural diffidence evoked caution on greasy corners in the wet. Once or twice I caught the back end trying to step out, but I think that was more to do with a residue of spilled diesel after a shower. Otherwise it clung limpet-like in any situation, and in town its prodigious traction and lightness proved to be a bonus. On more than one occasion I found myself making several circuits of roundabouts just for the hell of it, and the Elise just revelled in being hurtled round and round. You get dizzy before the car wants to stop playing.

My wife, Laura, admired its performance too. 'It's a superb car for a cross-country run,' she said. 'And taking off from traffic lights is just brilliant. If I was single and still lived in London it would be exactly my cup of tea. But it runs out of steam at about 100; there isn't the reserve of power you've got with our Alfa.' Other pals who got to have a ride also saw it as a second car for high days and holidays. Brilliant fun they thought, but not your everyday transport. There's no pleasing some people!

SPARTAN COCKPIT

The Elise windscreen provides you with an optimistic picture of the weather, because the top couple of inches are tinted sky blue. The interior of the car is a spartan environment, partly because of the need to

The austere, no-frills cockpit focuses concentration on driving aptitude.

save weight and partly because the design just looks clean that way. There's a refreshing purity about the bare, uncarpeted aluminium chassis defining the fabric of the interior.

Getting in and out of sports cars has always involved a certain amount of unnatural contortions and an absence of false modesty. As we know, the Elise was originally conceived as a step-in car, which might have made access easier. Or it might not. In any case, it's not a difficult car to get into, no more so than a Caterham, for example. For any of the uninitiated who might care to know before taking a ride, here's how to get out of the car. You push yourself up (from the driving seat) using the side of the passenger seat to obtain leverage; get your right leg out, holding onto the steering wheel with your left hand while your right hand supports your weight on the sill. When your right foot is on the ground, bring your left leg over so you're sitting on the sill, and lift yourself out. It's all a matter of experimentation until you hit on the optimum route.

Here's a second opinion, from my wife:

> You cannot drive this car if you're wearing a skirt. You just can't get into it with any modesty, and that's a real issue for women. Although it does feel safe inside – you're almost lying down – it's cosy and almost womb-like. It's pretty inside as well as out, the way you get the mix of metal and colour is really nice.

Inside the cockpit all the controls are well laid out, and everything is at your fingertips. The distance between the steering wheel and the gear lever is about 3in (75mm). The light stalk and two-speed wiper switches are right where you need them, and the window winder is just 6in (150mm) from the wheel. The light buttons

Access to the cockpit is tighter with the top on, but once the art of entry has been mastered it is no problem – but women are advised to wear trousers in the interests of modesty!

are activated by a single push. There's an integrated electronic speedo and tachometer system by Stack instruments with multifunction LCD display, and the dials come over as appropriately minimalist. The speedo is on the right, the rev-counter on the left; and the speedo is calibrated in mph and km/h. There are warning lights under the speedometer, and below the rev-counter are the fuel and temperature symbols.

The digital petrol gauge read 75 litres when the car was full, and diminished accordingly, while the temperature gauge was running at 86°C in normal running. The omnipresent cooling fan turned itself off with the ignition. The mileometer and trip are in a little space to the left, and all are housed in the single binnacle, all clearly visible through the top half of the steering wheel. The radio aerial is mounted behind the rear window, and in case you have a stereo fitted by your dealer, Lotus supply a couple of trim sections to go either

With engine cover raised to expose the 1.8-litre K-series twin-cam motor, the luggage bay is also accessible. It is just adequate for a decent-sized hold-all.

side of it on the dash panel.

In order to hold the engine cover up, you simply prop it open with the luggage compartment cover, although how you then work on the engine is not clear. Luggage space is better than you might expect, and there's room for a reasonable-sized holdall or smallish suitcase. Space is diminished by the need to accommodate the soft-top when it's removed. The cant rails and cross bars stow away neatly enough behind the seats, and if you were pushed for space, then the hood could probably be tucked

away there too. There's also a net behind the seats to enclose other small personal effects so they don't fly around when you're on the move.

TOPS OFF

It's always fun to drive a sports car with the top off, although it was never an imposition to drive it with the rag roof in place. In fact, travelling at anything like 100mph (160km/h) with the top off started

The cant rails are tapered towards the front end, where there is a ball fitting that pops into the windscreen header rail, and a neat little clip at the back end. The poppers that the canopy's press studs push onto can be seen on the inside of the cant rail.

The author takes his time to assemble the hood frame, inserting the cross-braces into the cant rails on either side. Even during a downpour the operation cannot be hurried.

to feel rather uncomfortable, presumably because the aerodynamics were distorted by the open cockpit, and the car developed a certain twitchiness. Far better to go topless motoring in a relaxed cruising mode. Besides, you can hold a conversation in the fresh air at 60mph (100km/h), but much faster than that it becomes a shouting match.

It rained quite a lot during the test periods with both cars – one in the early spring, the other in high summer – but the roof never showed any signs of leaking (until my very last day with the yellow car – see below), which is a major bonus.

It's easier to describe how to assemble the hood than how to take it down. So, assuming you've started with the top off, to put it up you first need the cant rails that pass down either side, between roll hoop and A-pillar, just above the side windows. These cant rails are tapered towards the front, and have a ball fitting that pops into the windscreen header rail, while the back end has a neat little clip.

You hold the cant rail and apply a little bit of pressure by leaning into the windscreen, and the clip at the rear fits into its housing on the door shut. The cant rails are braced by two virtually flat hoops that pass from side to side across the car, and they spring-fit into place. Then you take the hood itself and cast it over the lattice frame you've just created. A plastic fillet runs along the leading edge of the hood, and you slide that under the ridge along the length of the windscreen header rail. It's best to start with the corner sections, which are separated from the major part of it. This fixture is actually very efficient, although in character it reminded me of my Elan S4 back in the 1970s, where, as I've said before, the top was prone to blow itself off at speed because a similar hood-to-header rail

fitting proved to be inadequate.

When you are satisfied that the front is flush, you can pop the chrome spikes at the rear into the receptacles provided in the flying buttresses. At the sides, poppers press on to fixings in the cant rails inside the cockpit. Finally, you return to the rear and tension the whole canopy by means of a pair of Allen bolts set in the spikes using the key provided. This little tool has a home in the rear bulkhead just behind the driver's seat.

The Elise top is not a quick bit of kit to erect, however. To do it at a leisurely pace can take maybe five minutes, and there's none of the 'up and down at the traffic lights' stuff that you can do with an Alfa Romeo Spider or an MGB. It's a bit more sophisticated than a Morgan or Caterham, with their antiquated lift-a-dot type fasteners, but an indication of the absolute fastest it could be put on was carried out when I returned the car to Hethel. A storm had been brewing all afternoon, but the children insisted on travelling in top-down mode for the final fling. Having arrived at the Lotus sentry box, the heavens opened. And as huge hail stones bounced stingingly off my bald head, we hustled the framework of rods and rails together, flinging the canopy over like crazed campers wrestling with a fly-sheet. The whole operation was managed in just under three minutes, which can hardly be described as slick when that's the best you can do under pressure.

Thus, drenched and battered, my affair with the orange Elise drew to a close. I parted company with the yellow car under similar, although not such sodden conditions, as I didn't have to get the top back on. This time, though, I discovered how important it is to have the canopy aligned absolutely symmetrically across the windscreen header rail. It might have looked all right, but closer examination revealed that I'd fitted the hood fractionally out of true, and a small but steady trickle of water dripped into the car from the top left corner. I am pleased to note, however, that the single blade of the two-speed wiper cleared water most effectively from the screen during the accompanying downpour.

As I say, the yellow car was hardly run in, and it was my privilege to be the first writer to drive it. As well as confirming impressions formed with the first car, it showed just how tight the drivetrain is before all and sundry have mauled it around at Millbrook or wherever. Its functions were crisper and it was even more delightful to operate than the orange machine. Lotus PR man Alastair Florance pointed out one or two revisions, which included the mandatory smaller-diameter tail pipes set within the original chrome ones, and the combined radio and portable phone aerial behind the rear screen.

The most significant departure from the original spec was the cast iron ventilated brake discs, fitted instead of the Brembo metal matrix variety. The difference seemed quite marked at first. The yellow car wasn't so prompt about slowing down as the orange car, and I felt there was less 'feel' about the cast iron disc-braked car. But if you applied enough pressure on the pedal, it stopped with no problem. I subsequently asked Dave Minter about this, and he confirmed that my impression had been right. Now it seems that metal matrix discs are destined for SE spec cars, while the standard model will get the cast iron jobs. Dave reckoned that in a road context the cast iron discs provide a bit of 'squeezability', whereas the MMC discs are perhaps 'wooden' in feel.

The yellow car was also one of the first batch to be painted with the water-based paint, and it contained an element of mica to produce a slight metallic effect – only really discernible in sunlight. There was some debate about what to call this colour, although 'new mustard' seemed the favourite. For some reason, people associate Lotuses with the colour yellow,

The Elise heads the author's most wanted car list. Here, with headlights and driving lights ablaze, Lotus PRO Pruneliar Stuart takes the press car for a run in the Norfolk countryside for the benefit of Beaulieu lensman Tom Wood.

Laura Tipler declared that the Elise is an ideal car for making fast cross-country trips, as well as being quickest off the mark at traffic lights.

although apart from the Camel-sponsored F1 cars and the GT1 sports racers there can't have been any real precedent. It may have been a popular colour for 1960s Elans and later Esprits perhaps, but I'd have said British racing green with yellow stripes was really traditional Lotus, though.

There's no doubt about it, the Elise is a real treat to drive, it's stunning to look at and it turns heads like a supercar. Overall, it is so brilliant that it currently heads my most wanted car list. But family considerations cloud my preferences, and I find myself wondering what a four-seater would be like – and I don't mean a beast like the Lotus Carlton. Lotus have shown in the past that they can produce an elegant package, with the Plus 2 Elan and the Excel, for instance. So even though the Elise coupé was shelved (for the time being), maybe there is a proper Lotus two-plus-two waiting in the wings.

8 The GT1 Sports Racing Car

The GT1 was a direct development of Elise technology, and was introduced for the 1997 season by Group Lotus International and the rather ambiguously named GTI Racing. There were two distinct versions: a road car, required for homologation purposes, and an all-out racing car. They were built in the old Team Lotus premises at Ketteringham Hall. The race project was designed by Martin Ogilvy (who was involved with the ground-effect Lotus 79 F1 car) and developed under the guidance of chief engineer George Howard Chappell, in order to contest the GT1 class of the BPR/FIA GT Series and endurance events, including the Le Mans 24-Hours. By way of background, Lotus had contested the BPR and GT2 championships in 1995 with an Esprit Sport 300, moving up to GT1 level the following year with an Esprit V8.

Detailed engineering and use of advanced materials achieved a target weight of 1,980lb (900kg), running with the GM-derived V8-engine, which produced over 550bhp in race tune. The incoming head of Lotus Design, Russell Carr, created the styling for a new body in carbon fibre. What emerged was the result of long hours of aerodynamic development in the wind tunnel, the object being to create a functional version of the Elise shape that would provide both stability and balance with minimum drag.

Given that the regular road-going Elise bore similar styling cues to certain sports racing cars of the 1960s, you might have expected that its racing form would look even more like a Ferrari P4 or Lola T70. But the GT1 didn't at all, being altogether flatter in aspect and featuring more air scoops and state-of-the-art aerodynamic skirts and spoilers. Its rear wing acted in conjunction with both the body and the underbody sections of the car to create substantial downforce. Cooling efficiency was also critical, to cope with the demands of running at high power for several hours in a variety of climates, and driver cooling – without air conditioning – for endurance racing was a vital consideration.

Venting for the rear brakes was provided by intakes at the front of the car, which channelled cool air down through the smooth inner surface of the chassis main beams directly onto the brake discs. Intakes at the side and rear of the car supplied cool air for engine oil and engine bay cooling as well as the engine air intakes at centre.

The original idea was to equip the GT1 with the Esprit's 3,506cc V8 (bore and stroke: 83mm x 81 mm), allied to twin Allied Signal intercooled turbochargers, and second-generation competition fuel injection and Lotus Racing EFI engine management systems. Development of the racing engine was carried out by Lotus Racing and Lotus Engineering during the 1996 season in the Esprit racing in the BPR Series. Drive was through a six-speed sequential Hewland gearbox, incorporating quick-change interchangeable ratios. An

AP Racing four-plate hydraulically operated clutch was used, similar to the specification of the 1996 Esprit V8 race car.

CHASSIS EVOLUTION

The chassis of the Lotus GT1 was an ingenious evolution of the Elise's extruded aluminium chassis, and the monocoque of the race car was reinforced through the installation of an integrated roll cage, which created a high level of torsional rigidity. Solid, fully rose-jointed racing suspension pick-ups provided highly accurate feedback, coupled with race specification Firth Rixson coil springs over Penske lightweight dampers. Competition wheels were Speedline cast magnesium, 18in in diameter, 11in wide at the front and 13in wide at the rear.

Brakes were AP competition six-piston machined aluminium callipers front and rear, with 14in cast iron discs, or the option of Carbon Industrie carbon brakes of the same diameter. The driver actuated adjustable brake balance control as required. Tyres fitted on the road version were Michelin Pilot MXX3. The air jacking system was a three-point set-up with two jacks at the rear and the third located under the nose of the car, with the compressed air plug point located by the right-hand front lower windscreen.

Engine bay of the road-going GT1, showing the Lotus-designed Corvette LT5 V8 motor, and the fully rose-jointed suspension with Firth Rixson coil springs over Penske lightweight dampers.

The racing version of the GT1 sports different rear view mirror and a rear aerofoil. The front splitter has an extra lip on it to further enhance the aerodynamics.

In the event, all was not to go smoothly, however. GTI Racing began the 1997 season at a severe disadvantage when regulations for turbocharged engines were abruptly changed to the detriment of the team very shortly before the start of the championship. Unsettled by the pace set by the turbocharged Porsche 911 GT1 in 1996, the sport's ruling body legislated turbos out of contention, and this ruling effectively made the powerful, efficient and reliable Lotus 918 3.5-litre V8 twin-turbo engine uncompetitive. A new 6.0-litre normally aspirated engine based on the Chevrolet Corvette motor was hurriedly developed in record time for the start of the season.

Then, in early summer, the difficulties were compounded when engine regulations reverted back to those of 1996. It seemed that influential lobbying from Stuttgart had persuaded the FIA to change its mind. This made it impossible for the GTI Team to turn in consistent results and meant that the full potential of the Type 115 could not be exploited.

In October 1997 Lotus went on record as having 'grave reservations about the future of FIA GT Championship'. The company stated that it was pulling out of the series, and would instead channel its resources into expanding and developing its core business activities. The arrangement with GTI Racing broke up in acrimonious litigation, however, as Group Lotus terminated the agreement with GTI Racing Ltd, who retained the cars. GTI team manager Ian Foley remained upbeat about the future of the team, saying: 'Although we've finished an exciting period with Lotus, we've developed a superb car with them and we're still committed to offering support and development services to existing Type 115 customers.' The motor racing press tended to refer to the car as the Elise GT1, because they still wanted to associate Lotus with the sport.

During the 1997 season the works GT1s were driven by the Dutch duo Jan Lammers partnered by Mike Hezemans (son of 1960s Touring Car champion Toine, who ran the GTI Racing team), and Frenchmen Fabien Giroix and Jean-Denis Deletraz. Two other GT1s were raced, a French one in Benetton colours and another in the German national GT series.

In competition the 6.0-litre V8's high fuel consumption necessitated too many refuelling stops, which negated some high qualifying advantages over the Porsche 911 GT1s.

Lotus were not alone in their disenchantment with the race series. Ferrari, McLaren, and TVR all effectively pulled out of what had looked a highly promising show back in 1996, leaving a two-horse race between the pastiche GT cars of Porsche and Mercedes-Benz. However, the exercise did demonstrate what was possible as a spin off from Elise chassis technology.

PARALLEL LINES

I discussed the creation of the road-going GT1 with project manager Neil Lloyd and chassis and technical designer Richard Rackham.

Neil: We were based down in the chapel at Ketteringham Hall because it was felt we could operate there without too many distractions. The programme was initiated by GTI Racing, and both road and race engineers worked in the same drawing office because there was so much interchange of requirements – for example, race regulations demanded certain types of bodywork, which we had to have on the road car. It was very complicated, developing two subtly different cars in parallel, when in fact the goals were mutually exclusive. There was also an incredibly demanding time scale, and it was the only way we were going to get the race car ready for next season, basically. The project was suggested in June 1996, and our absolute deadline was 14 April 1997.

There were many long working days, no holidays and not a lot of sleep for the ten members of the core GT1 road car team. Other specialist talents, like laminators, came and went during the programme, and Romano Artioli was a passionately enthusiastic visitor. He even described to Russell Carr how he thought the front air ducts should look.

Clearly the foregoing race programme with the Esprit had given Lotus staff a taste of the racing lifestyle and technology, which stood them in good stead and provided an understanding of race team thinking, as opposed to mainstream – albeit low volume – manufacture. But as orders go, they don't come much taller.

Neil: We had ten months to carry out a styling exercise, an engineering design and development programme, and then test it. We started with a road version of the turbocharged Elise V8, so it was a known quantity. We tried to carry over certain components and systems, like the screen and wiper, in order to reduce development time. The renderings and modelling for the body were started in July 1996, going through that autumn. During that winter in December the racing car was doing some shakedown testing, and the road car was ready shortly after that, in mid-January 1997.

Richard: The objective was to have a competitive race car, so we had to see what was being designed for the race car and interpret that the best was for the road car to go through homologation. There were some vast differences. I think they had 450bhp and could be as noisy as they liked, whereas the road car had the V8 Esprit engine, and it had to comply with the 74-

decibel drive-line noise requirement. So the exhaust system had to contain two silencers from the standard Esprit in series, and we mounted an entirely different inlet on the centre of the roof, because the microphone for the drive-by noise test is actually on the side of the car. Because the tyres make a lot of noise we had to have grooved tyres, and they were shaved to the point where they would be as quiet as possible. And we had noise suppressant over the inside of the bodyshell.

In order to save money in the programme the race team asked for a racing gearbox to

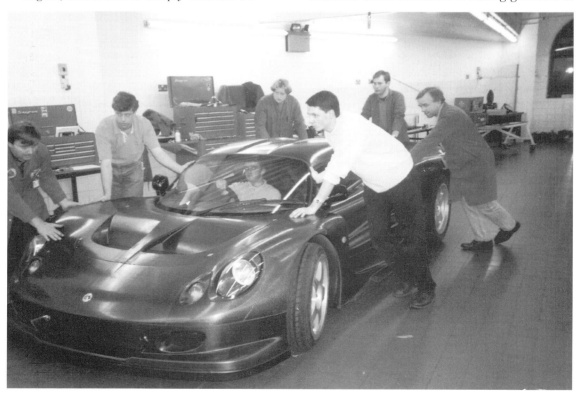

The GT1 road car is wheeled out of the Ketteringham workshops for the first time. It's fairly obvious that it's altogether broader than the regular Elise. At the wheel is road car No 1 mechanic Richard Walton, with project manager Neil Lloyd on the right of the car and liaison engineer Steve Hubnut to the left.

be installed in the road car – much against Lotus Engineering's advice – as they believed it would be quiet enough. In practice the straight-cut gears in the solidly mounted gearbox proved to be far too loud. The quick fix was to use rubber mounts for the drivetrain and switch to a standard Esprit gearbox (containing racing ratios), just in order to pass the drive-by noise requirements. They had to comply with emissions legislation and publish relevant figures too, despite conflicting objectives.

> Neil: We could have arrived at a more elegant solution, given more time and more investment in the project, but because of the time factor we couldn't afford a fail, so everything was belt-and-braces.
>
> Richard: We tried to carry as much over from the Elise so we could more easily pass a piece of paper to the authorities to get the road-going version homologated. They had to get all the homologation documentation passed by the 14 April deadline in order to get the race car on the grid. The homologation papers were literally flown to the race circuit and placed into the scrutineers' hands.

It was an incredible achievement to produce the road and race cars in just ten and a half months, and to present the homologation documents with just two hours to go was worthy of Chapman's halcyon days.

'At that point it was done and dusted as far as we were concerned,' said Neil. Before then, however, the two cars were developing in parallel, and while the race car was much purer in terms of aerodynamics, the road car had rather different requirements.

> Richard: But there were tremendous changes to the Elise road car. For example, the chassis rails at the back of the car were 150mm longer, although the bends were the same. They used an adhesive with a higher temperature capability, and the longer rear section enabled the V8 engine to fit in longitudinally. Everything was mounted solidly in the chassis, which is normal race car procedure. Obviously the suspension both front and rear had to be much stronger, with a wider track.

Although it was known as the Elise GT1, about the only thing it had in common with the road car was the chassis. From the seating position, the bodywork and cooling system to the brakes and drivetrain, everything was new on the race prototype. Inside was a very substantial steel roll cage, which not only provided driver protection, but also stiffened the shell to a huge degree, allowing the rock-hard racing suspension to do its job properly. The stiffer the springs are, the stiffer the structure needs to be.

Certain aspects that we tend to take for granted also needed to be addressed. For instance, the racing car didn't need any lights, but the road car had to have a higher ride height so that its lights complied with the 500mm minimum dip-beam height regulations. This also meant that the race car had different dampers from the road car, which needed much more suspension travel to gain the greater ride height, while the racing car had virtually no suspension travel at all. The geometry of the suspension set-up was different as well. The road car required a handbrake and the racer did not, and of course the race car had to be equipped with a much larger fuel tank with a rubber fuel cell. The Stack instrument pack used on the Elise was not appropriately calibrated for the racer.

The GT1 road car was given its shakedown by John Miles, who contemplates its austere cockpit prior to taking it onto the Hethel test track.

Richard: One of the lucky breaks was the Reg. 12 crash test. Because the Elise had passed it with flying colours and there had been no movement outside the 5in (125mm) limit, we were able to extrapolate the results from the Elise into the GT1. We said that although the GT1 weighs one and a half times as much as the Elise, we still think the steering wheel will move less than the 5in. The authorities accepted that, and we didn't have to crash a car, which was very fortunate as we'd have had to build two cars in order to crash one of them.

Neil: The absolute essential there was that we shouldn't exceed our weight target, because if we had, we couldn't extrapolate the data and we would have had to crash a car. So it was important that the design engineers bore this in mind. Again, two silencers were not the way to go to meet a weight target.

The compromises built in to the road car meant that at first it was virtually undriveable. This was because the clutch was a racing variety, which is like an on-off switch.

Richard: It just takes up and you shoot off. It had got what amounted to a switch for a clutch, coupled with a soft-mounted engine and transmission that we ended up with to satisfy the drive-by noise requirements. And when you let the clutch up, it was all drama. It bit with such ferocity that the engine jumped about and smacked everything at the back of the structure. It took a lot of skill to actually get it moving, but luckily it settled down once you'd got the clutch up and your eyeballs had adjusted to the sensation!

Neil: It was a very unfriendly thing to drive in terms of refinement. And naturally its performance was quite staggering, bearing in mind it was basically an Elise with just a bit of extra weight. I've never driven anything like it. Your senses were completely bombarded with sensations – the heat, the smell, vibrations. As a working environment it was bad, until the engine was soft mounted.

At this point they were still talking about the original engine configuration, the 3.5-litre unit with twin turbos.

This is the homologation special, the roadgoing version of the GT1, which has a taller ride height than the race-car. Competition wheels are 18in diameter Speedline cast magnesium, 11in wide at the front and 13in wide at the rear.

Neil: We were running an engine with just a bit more power delivery as a standard Esprit. It was a different-looking engine from the standard unit, though, and the engine management system was different. When they were obliged to switch from hard mountings to soft, it became necessary to reintroduce certain features from the standard Esprit engine, like injecting clean air into the exhaust to cause less pollution. The race car didn't have that, and it involved modifying inlet and exhaust manifolding and installing blower pumps.

There was no respite from the regulations: the road car had to be homologated like any other road-going vehicle. It had run at Ketteringham Hall, and at first it ran only intermittently when it arrived at the factory, typically late one January night. John Miles got the job of giving it the first shakedown test to prove it was a runner, after which it was a matter of refining all the systems in order to pass the legislation tests. At Hethel it was fine-tuned on the rolling road and checked on emissions and drive-by noise testing equipment, not to mention the test track. Once it had passed through those facilities Lotus could go into legislation testing with some degree of confidence.

> Neil: After that, the focuses changed, and the racing team split away to follow a programme to find more performance with reliability. They were in pursuit of more brake horsepower with more downforce, while we were after lower emissions and lower noise levels, so from then onwards we were following mutually exclusive goals.

The abrupt decision to run with the 6.0-litre V8 engine was based on the fact that some of Lotus's powertrain people like Alan Nobbs had experience with the LT5 Corvette engine, and race results from the USA showed it was capable of producing the sort of power required to run in the BPR series. Alan had been in charge of the engine programme for the racing Esprits, and with the Esprit V8 engine in its final form he had finally achieved reliability. One of the main reasons for undertaking the GT1 programme was because a more aerodynamic shape was wanted. The Esprit's flat screen renders it aerodynamically poor, whereas the Elise's curved screen is more like those of the McLaren F1 and Porsche 911 derivative. And had the GT1 class of the championship become more focused, as had been anticipated, it would have challenged Formula 1 for performance and spectacle, and the Esprit would have lagged even more behind, so there was another reason to develop the new car.

But to an extent Nobbs was trying to achieve the impossible with the GT1 programme. When the regulations changed, it threw the racing team into some disarray, as the 6.0-litre unit is a much bigger engine and required changes to the chassis cross-beams and bulkhead. It

was necessary to source some of the components like cams and valves and tuning equipment for the engine from the USA before it could be run on the dynamometer to make it reliable. It was the tenacious Alan Nobbs who went to the US specially to acquire them, and the tuning and setting up was done over the Christmas period.

DOUBLE WHAMMY

> Richard: They caught a double whammy, because the regulations were changed back again and Lotus were uncompetitive. So maybe they changed their effort prematurely, and they set themselves an impossible target. Companies like Porsche and Mercedes have literally shelves of engines all ready and waiting for such eventualities, and it's no problem for them. They'll have done numerous dyno tests and optimized engine sizes to comply with regulation changes and different circuits even.

But there was another issue to take into account.

> Neil: While this was happening to the race car, we had to give some consideration to whether or not it could be made to work as a road-going derivative. Because if you compete successfully for a season you'd have to seriously consider producing the road-going variant, or else risk losing all your points. So there was a real conflict here, because the Esprit engine was homologated in the road car, whereas the 6.0-litre installation was not. Anyone who was racing a turbo V8-powered GT1 was fine, but the normally aspirated cars were at the mercy of the race series organizers. But although that never happened, there

The GT1 made its debut at the 1997 Racing Car Show, but potential success on the track was thwarted by regulation changes.

could have been penalties imposed for the 1998 season.

Richard: We put a lot of work into making the road car look nice. The packaging of the engine bay was sorted out so that if we did ever sell it as a road car it would be attractive.

The GT1 road car's fate was to be sold off by GTI Racing at an auction at the Monaco Grand Prix. Lotus never actually owned the car, and were acting in the capacity of engineering consultants during the build

and development period, so GTI Racing had the rights to both road and race cars. But had the cars been a runaway success in the race series, it is likely that a small run of GT1 derivatives would have been produced. As it was, it probably wouldn't have appealed to collector, as it was so close to a race car. Comparisons? I recalled driving a Ford RS200 Group B rally car and that was pretty raw. Richard and Neil thought a GT40 might be nearer the mark. Now there's an icon to match it with.

Lotus GT1 Dimensions (in/mm)

Length	177/4,495
Width	81.5/2.070
Height	43/1,100
Ground Clearance	120mm
Wheelbase	105/2,675
Front Track	67/1,700
Rear Track	65/1,643
Kerb Weight	1,980lb (900kg)

9 Evolutions

THE ELISE 340R

The Elise 340R first appeared on the Lotus stand at the NEC Motor Show on 20 October 1998. The 340R takes the Elise concept to the extreme, and my first reaction was that it was just a concept car, a prototype that wouldn't make it to production. But Lotus PR officer Alastair Florance said that they definitely would productionize it. The prototype weighed little more than 500kg and was powered by a 170bhp K-series engine that provided a power-to-weight ratio of 340bhp per ton – from which it derives its name, or number if you prefer. Like the Elise that sired it, the 340R was promoted as a track car that can also be used on public roads.

The fruits of Lotus Engineering and Lotus Design, the 340R concept was summed up in this way by its designer, Russell Carr:

> We decided to develop a road-going race car that would be even more elemental than the Elise, solely focused on providing pure driving pleasure. We wanted a car that would embody the same Lotus characteristics as the Elise, but even more innovative, lightweight, elegant and fun to drive.

The front headlights were faired into the top of the bodyshell, enhancing its aerodynamic qualities, while the drivetrain and Motad sports exhaust was almost entirely revealed by a lack of bodywork at the rear. In the absence of a panel to house

them in, the rear lights and indicators projected on stalks. Twin interlocked roll-over hoops crowned distinctive blue and red bucket seats like gothic arches, and the Yokohama-shod alloy wheels were covered – just – by composite cycle mudguards to further promote the competition car theme. These could be removed for track use, and whether fully exposed or not, the driver would have an unencumbered view of the position and orientation of the wheels and tyres, for precise placement of the car in corners.

The initial mock-up was built around a crashed Elise chassis, but the prototype shown at the NEC was assembled using all-new components. Adaptations to the Elise chassis for the new model were carried out by Richard Rackham, and it was clad in carbon fibre and composite panels. The single-piece, doorless bodyshell top was designed to be completely removable, providing easy access to major mechanical components. The chassis and powertrain were encased by bodywork only where absolutely necessary for driver comfort and safety, or aerodynamic efficiency. Two removable inspection covers in the recess of the front radiator and one at the rear of the vehicle provided access for checking fluid levels.

Although the 340R prototype shown at the NEC was fitted with the standard 118hp Rover K-series motor and standard gearbox, Lotus expected to use a road-legal version the VHPD (Very High Power Derivative) engine for the production car. Its 170bhp was attained at 8000rpm, with a high torque of 142Nm at 5000 rpm. Like the Elise Sport, the engine would be linked to an ultra close ratio straight-cut gear box, which would give the driver an opportunity to exploit the potential of a race engine to the full.

The 340R also used Koni Racing two-way adjustable dampers, adjustable for both bump and rebound with higher spring rates, together with a stiffer front anti-roll bar. The 340R was displayed at Birmingham with hand-cut Yokohama slicks and ultra-light magnesium O.Z. F1 wheels, but the eventual production version would use a soft-compound road-legal tyre developed by Yokohama in close conjunction with Lotus ride and handling engineers.

Braking was provided by four-pot AP Racing callipers with 295mm-diameter drilled and ventilated discs at the front, and AP Racing callipers on 282mm drilled and ventilated discs at the rear.

Adjustability

Because of its road and track designation, a degree of adjustability was designed into the car. The driver could alter both the suspension setting and the rake of the rear wing to produce the most ideal set-up for any particular environment. Further aerodynamic downforce was provided by the powerful underbody rear diffuser and the top exit radiator, which ducts air up

Unveiled at the 1998 NEC Motor Show, the 340R was an even more pared-down version of the Elise.

through the front radiator over the cut-down windscreen, thus creating a net downforce at the front of the car.

In the cockpit, the lightweight composite racing seats were trimmed in vinyl and alcantara, and allied to four-point racing harnesses. The adjustable driver's seat was located towards the centre-line of the car, with the removable passenger seat fixed in the rearmost position.

Steering was by an offset, quick release Momo wheel, and the pedals were the same extruded aluminium variety as the Elise.

The centre console contained what Russell Carr described as 'jewel-like' technical detail. A trendy push-button starter accompanied the twin-cowled Stack racing instrument pack, with an integrated DAS (Data Acquisition System) for downloading data from the electronic instruments directly onto a PC. Creature comforts in the 340R didn't extend to a heater, and instead the driver's visibility was assured by an invisible electric heating element in the windscreen.

The 340R prototype was finished in DuPont-developed high-tech paint, and in titanium and black this blend of pigment and glass bead lacquer provided an aptly futuristic finish. It was a little late arriving, but the original idea for the Elise project had finally materialized, for here was that oft-discussed creature, the step-in-car. It had made it after all.

For racing purposes the driver could alter suspension and rear wing settings on the 340R.

Lotus Elise 340R

Engine

Type	Four cylinders in line, transverse mid-mounted
Capacity	1796 cc
Construction	Aluminium engine block with aluminium cylinder head
Power	170bhp at 8000rpm
Torque	142Nm at 5000rpm
Bore/Stroke	80 mm x 89.3 mm
Valves	Double overhead camshaft with mechanical tappets
Fuelling	Fuel injected
Alternator	85A

Transmission Manual five-speed transaxle driving rear wheels, hydraulic clutch.

Body
Composite body panels with detachable one-piece top shell and integral fixed faired headlamps.

Chassis
Lotus-designed spaceframe structure of epoxy-bonded sections of aluminium extrusions (built by Hydro Aluminium) incorporating dedicated integral occupant roll-over protection.

Suspension
Double wishbones with over two-way adjustable single coil springs and Koni monotube dampers all round. Lotus-patented uprights of extruded aluminium, made by Alusuisse.

Steering
Rack and pinion, no power assistance.

Wheels

Type	Ultra-light magnesium wheels made for Lotus by OZ Racing
Front	16in x 7in
Rear	17in x 8in

Tyres

Type	Yokohama A038
Front	195/45 x 16
Rear	25/40 x 17

Brakes
Non-servo split hydraulic system
Front four-pot AP Racing callipers with 95mm diameter drilled and ventilated disks.
Rear AP Racing callipers with 82mm drilled and ventilated disks at the rear.

Instrumentation
Stack analogues electronic unit with DAS (Data Acquisition System) comprising speedometer and tachometer with multifunction LCD readout incorporating fuel and coolant gauges.

Performance

Maximum speed	133mph (214km/h)
0–60 mph	4.0sec
0–100 mph	10.0sec

Dimensions (in/mm)	
Wheelbase	90.6/2,300
Overall length	137.8/3,500
Overall width	67.7/1,720
Overall height	41.3/1,050
Ground clearance	3.9/1.050
Fuel tank capacity	40 ltr/8.8gal
Fuel grade	98 RON minimum
Unladen weight	1,103 lb (500kg)
Weight distribution	3961 (% front/rear)

THE 111S – MORE OF THE SAME

When Rover made its MGF available with a supercharged 200bhp power unit in 1999, it could countenance the supply of 143bhp VVC K-series engines to Lotus for installation in the Elise. The evolution was just as dramatic as the Sprint version of the S4 Elan of 1970, and the word 'Sprint' seemed like a suitable designation for the VVC model. However, since other manufacturers had colonized the 'Sprint' title, they simply decided to use the Elise's factory type number instead, which was 111S. At its launch at the Geneva Show in March 1999, it was anticipated that the 111S version would account for at least half of all Elise sales.

Since its introduction in 1996, Lotus had offered tuned versions of the original F-series engine, while one or two after-market converters promised 150bhp from the basic 1.8-litre engine. The 1.8-litre K-series VVC engine was a sixteen-valve dohc unit using the same block as the standard engine but fitted with a more sophisticated head that featured variable valve control. This creates a continuously variable cam-lobe profile that alters the duration of the inlet valve opening and its phasing, according to both engine speed and loading, for optimum performance throughout the

With the 143bhp VVC K-Series engine fitted, the Elise was designated the 111S.

Main external differences on the 111S were the rear wing, wider wheels and tyres at the back, and headlamp fairings.

rev-range. The engine management system allows VVC to achieve a healthy power output at high revs, and at the same time maintain a decent amount of torque at lower engine speeds. The VVC unit had larger inlet and exhaust valves, a new inlet manifold and plenum chamber with increased flow capacities, all designed to improve engine breathing. It was fitted with full sequential fuel injection with adaptive control, and distributor-less ignition with individual coils for each cylinder.

For Lotus, fitting the VVC engine was also an opportunity to upgrade the Elise in other ways, with improvements calculated to justify a price increase of about £4,000 over the basic model, which in 1999 was £22,450, making the VVC-engined version £26,500. Top speed was raised to 133mph, and the 0–60mph dash was covered in 5.38sec, with 100mph coming up in 14.4sec. The 111S weighed in at 15kg heavier than the standard Elise.

Although the performance figures suggest that standing-start acceleration is not dramatically improved, in practice the variable valve timing makes the VVC engine feel much more eager, and this is matched by a set of lower, close-ratio gears and modified final drive, which makes mid-range acceleration somewhat brisker. In practical terms it is thus a quicker car to drive on fast A- and B-roads, and Dave Minter reckoned that with the close ratio gearbox it had even more of the feel of a track car since it could stay in the power band during hard driving. The changes were not made lightly, with months of testing spent on track and the open road to achieve the desired result. It's what they do best, after all. Yet at the end of the day it boils down to the size of your bank balance as to whether the increased performance is worth the extra cash; the basic car is already so good. However, there's more to it than that.

The other 'improvements' that Lotus has made include new, wider 7.5J six-spoke O.Z. wheels shod with broader and therefore more tenacious rear tyres than the original P-Zeros – up from 205- to 225-width – with revised toe-steer angles to suit the broader rubber. Cosmetically, the perspex headlamp covers that were fitted on the prototypes made a comeback, the front grille was new and the front indicator lenses received a smoked effect. But apart from a bulge on the engine cover that accommodates the VVC engine's valve-gear, possibly the most obvious way to recognize the 111S is by its rear wing. Internally, there are more significant improvements. Having complained about the seats in the standard car, there are now properly padded seats upholstered in leather. Although your backside is more inclined to slide around on leather than on fabric-covered seats, there is a distinct lift about the value-added quality of leather, which is arguably more durable as well. The new seat design was standardized for all Elise models, along with new metal window winders and carbon-effect trim on the facia. Whatever evolution we're talking about, the Elise formula is spot-on, and that hasn't been lost on the major players. Another concept car unveiled at the Geneva Show was by Lotus Engineering's client General Motors, whose 147bhp 2.2-litre two-seater Speedster was built for GM by Lotus and based on an Elise chassis. But regrettably, since it lacked the external grace and charm of the donor model, the prospects for a mass-market Elise-class sports car for those on a more limited budget doesn't look likely.

Lotus Elise 111S (1999)

Body
Composite body panels with detachable front and rear clamshells and rear wing; integral headlamps with aerodynamic faired lens covers; spats toaccommodate wider tyres. Clamshell weights: front 13.3kg, rear 15.3kg.

Chassis
Lotus-designed spaceframe structure of twenty-six different epoxy-bonded sections of 6063 Aluminium Silicon Alloy extrusions (built by Hydro Aluminium) incorporating integral roll-over hoop. Weight 68kg. Torsional stiffness 10133 Nm/degree.

Suspension
Double wishbones with single coil springs over Koni monotube dampers all round. Lotus-patented uprights of extruded aluminium, made by Alusuisse.

Steering
Rack and pinion; ratio: 15.8:1

Wheels
Type	Unique Lotus-designed 6-spoke, by O.Z.
Front	5.5J x 15
Rear	7.5J x 16

Tyres
Type	Pirelli P Zero
Front	185/55 R15
Rear	225/45 R16

Brakes
282mm diameter cast iron cross-drilled ventilated discs, mounted outboard. Non-servo split hydraulic system, including unique Lotus/AP Racing opposed piston front callipers.

Instrumentation
Analogue electronic unit comprising speedometer and tachometer with multi-function LCD readout incorporating fuel and coolant gauges, supplied by Stack Instruments.

Engine
Cylinders	4 cylinders in line, mid mounted transversely
Capacity	1,796cc
Construction	Aluminium engine block with aluminium cylinder head
Max. power	143 bhp at 7,000 rpm
Max. torque	174 Nm at 4,500 rpm
Bore and stroke	80mm x 89.3mm
Valves	Double overhead camshaft; Variable Valve Control (VVC) with varying cam lobe profile
Fuelling	Multiport sequential fuel injection
Ignition	MEMS 2J (Rover/Motorola)
Alternator	12V85A

Transmission

Type	Manual 5-speed transaxle driving rear wheels, hydraulic clutch
First	2.923
Second	1.750
Third	1.307
Fourth	1.033
Fifth	0.848
Reverse	3.000
Final drive:	4.200

Lighting

6in main beam headlamps with perspex covers. Optional auxiliary driving lamps. Smoked clear lens front indicators with amber bulbs

Performance

Maximum speed	213km/h (133mph)
0–62 mph (0–100 km/h)	5.38-seconds.
0–100 mph (0–160 km/h)	14.4-seconds

Fuel Consumpton (mpg/ltr x 100 km)

Urban	28.5/9.9
Extra urban	47.9/6.9
Combined	48.7/7.3

Standard equipment

Alloy road wheels (lockable), 3-way catalytic converter, coded signal immobilizer, vinyl hood, unique Lotus/Nardi steering wheel.

Dimensions

Wheelbase	90.6/2300
Front track	56.7/1440
Rear track	157.6/1465
Overall length	114.7/3734
Overall width	67.0/1701 (excluding mirrors)
Overall height	147.3/1202
Ground clearance	16.3/160
Fuel tank capacity	8.8 gal (40ltr)
Fuel grade	95 RON minimum
Dry Weight	1671 lb (714kg)
Unladen weight	1894 lb (770kg)
Weight distribution	39/61 (% front/rear)

Options

Standard	Cloth hood, storage pockets, passenger footrest, driving lamps,
Cost Options	Metallic paint, radio fitting kit, leather trim seats, Thatcham One approved Cobra alarm/immobilizer.

Index